M000189344

THE EQUAL PARENT PRESUMPTION

The Equal Parent Presumption

Social Justice
in the Legal Determination of
Parenting after Divorce

EDWARD KRUK

McGill-Queen's University Press
Montreal & Kingston • London • Ithaca

© McGill-Queen's University Press 2013

ISBN 978-0-7735-4291-4 (cloth)
ISBN 978-0-7735-9009-0 (ePDF)
ISBN 978-0-7735-9010-6 (ePUB)

Legal deposit fourth quarter 2013
Bibliothèque nationale du Québec

Printed in Canada on acid-free paper that is 100% ancient forest free
(100% post-consumer recycled), processed chlorine free

This book has been published with the help of a grant from the Canadian
Federation for the Humanities and Social Sciences, through the Awards to
Scholarly Publications Program, using funds provided by the Social Sciences
and Humanities Research Council of Canada.

McGill-Queen's University Press acknowledges the support of the Canada
Council for the Arts for our publishing program. We also acknowledge
the financial support of the Government of Canada through the Canada
Book Fund for our publishing activities.

Library and Archives Canada Cataloguing in Publication

Kruk, Edward, author
  The equal parent presumption: social justice in the legal
determination of parenting after divorce / Edward Kruk.

  Includes bibliographical references and index.
  Issued in print and electronic formats.
  ISBN 978-0-7735-4291-4 (bound). – ISBN 978-0-7735-9009-0 (ePDF). –
ISBN 978-0-7735-9010-6 (ePUB)

  1. Custody of children. 2. Children of divorced parents – Legal
status, laws, etc. 3. Divorce – Law and legislation. 4. Parent and child
(Law). 5. Parenting. 6. Social justice. I. Title.

K695.K78 2013   346.01'73   C2013-904013-7
                                          C2013-904014-5

This book was typeset by Interscript in 10/13 Sabon.

Contents

Acknowledgments

The subject of this book has been a preoccupation of mine since 1985. At that time, I embarked on PhD research examining why so many fathers became disengaged from their children's lives after divorce. My conclusion was that a legal decree of shared parenting would be the most effective measure to prevent what was in effect legally sanctioned parental alienation after divorce. Since that time, children's relationships with their parents generally have continued to erode in Canada – the result of misguided child and family policies – much to the detriment of children's well-being and healthy development.

Since that initial foray into divorce research, I have expanded my research focus to include mothers and children of divorce, divorce practitioners, and the impact of family law in the realm of contested child custody. The people who have assisted me in this lifetime effort are far too numerous to name, and I restrict myself to acknowledging those who have contributed to this book's development in the recent past.

First and foremost, thanks to legal scholar Natalie Nikolina of the Utrecht University School of Law, and to the entire international network of shared parenting scholars organized by Alexander Masardo at the University of Birmingham. Natalie's article, "The Influence of International Law on the Issue of Co-Parenting," was discussed by this group, and set the stage for the development of the first chapters of this book. I owe her a debt for her assistance in critiquing earlier drafts of this book, and for helping me to clarify key points. Her perspective as a scholar of international family law inspired me to set aside dominant discourses and antiquated thinking about child custody in favour of a new paradigm, that of co-parenting after divorce, which clarifies the meaning of "equal parenting."

The Honourable Anne Cools, Canadian Senator for Toronto Centre, cautions that in family law every case is individual, and that it is of paramount importance to define precisely "the best interests of children." The primary focus of this book thus remains the clarification of what constitutes the best interests of children in divorce. Following a tradition established by former Canadian Justice Minister Mark McGuigan, Senator Cools and others in the field of family justice during the Trudeau era have contributed significantly to our present-day understanding of family divorce. I thank the Senator for being a fighter for the interests of children in Canada, and particularly for hosting the Senate of Canada symposia on child and family policy in Canada over two decades.

I have been privileged to work with scholars such as Linda Nielsen of Wake Forest University, William Fabricius of Arizona State University, and Paul Millar of Nipissing University whose work in the arena of parenting after divorce and child custody determination has been enlightening. Equally influential are Paul Nathanson and Katherine Young of McGill University, who have asked some of the essential questions pertaining to what it means to be a parent and a human being. I also thank Barbara Kay for her insights and wisdom.

Finally, my thanks to Philip Cercone, Ryan Van Huijstee, and Gabrielle Zezulka of McGill-Queen's University Press, whose invaluable assistance helped bring this book to fruition.

Preface

The focus of this book is parenting after divorce and the best interests of children, in situations in which both parents are seeking to exclusively parent their children or are otherwise in conflict in regard to parenting after divorce. As such, the book will be of interest not only to divorce practitioners, policy-makers, academicians, and students, but also to parents themselves. After more than twenty-five years of studying the highly contentious issue of "child custody," my conclusion is that children of divorce will fare best if they are able to reside with each of their parents in an equal parenting arrangement, and that this key principle should be established as a presumption in law, and as fundamental to children's best interests and well-being. In the context of divorce, "equal parenting" may be defined along three dimensions:

1 Equality of power and influence such that neither party is able to control the other or is in a submissive position to the other, so that the faculty of free consent may be fully exercised by each parent. Equality of opportunity to actively parent is a key element in this regard.
2 Equality of the proportion of residential time spent by each parent with the child after divorce relative to the amount of time each parent spent with the child prior to divorce.
3 Equality of residential time spent with the child after divorce relative to the other parent (50% time division).

I will discuss how these three dimensions of gender equality are commensurate with a child-focused "best-interests-of-the-child-from-the-perspective-of-the-child" approach to the legal determination of child custody after divorce, and with a "responsibility-to-needs" approach to parenting after divorce.

In addition, I argue that the state has a fiduciary obligation to enable arrangements for healthy parenting after divorce. In this regard, the standard of living in all households in which a child resides should be sufficient to allow the child to have his or her essential needs met, ideally through the active parenting of both parents. The ongoing, direct involvement of parents in children's lives is vitally important to their well-being; the need for roots (Weil 1943) and family connectedness are the most neglected needs among children in contemporary society, and especially so in an era of new genetic technologies and redefinitions of "parent" in family law (Somerville 2006). Prevailing social policy in the Canadian child welfare field, including child protection and child care as well as child custody law and policy, serves largely to disconnect children from their families of origin (Neufeld and Mate 2004; Kruk 2011).

Systems of law based on antiquated "child custody" thinking are in decline, yet, in Canada, the present system of sole custody (referred to here as the "primary residence" or "primary parent" system) continues as the dominant policy, despite its demonstrated failure: it removes a parent as an active caregiver from a child's life, and gives rise to increased conflict and often first-time interpersonal violence. A viable option to this system exists, however; equal and shared parenting arrangements are associated with the active involvement of both parents and with diminished parental conflict, in both consensual and litigated divorces involving children. Tragically, one of the flaws of the present sole custody system is that child custody determination based on the discretionary "best-interests-of-the-child" principle is far from being an exact science, and judges make errors in judgment in deciding who will be the "primary caregiver." Equal and shared parental responsibility anchors a child in two households, and the chances that a child will receive the positive influence of at least one parent, when both parents are actively involved in the child's life, are vastly improved.

The aim of this book is to propose an evidence-based "best-interests-of-the-child-from-the-perspective-of-the-child" standard of child custody (or as I shall henceforth call it, parenting after divorce), to replace the present discretionary standard. That is, legal determination of post-divorce child caregiving arrangements should be primarily guided by the needs and interests of children, in line with the conclusions of current child-focused empirical research. This goal is best accomplished with an approach to the legal determination of children's best interests based on parents' "responsibility to needs" rather than their rights. An equal parenting presumption is most in keeping with an evidence-based, child-focused perspective of children's interests.

During the past two decades, the ideal of shared parenting responsibility for children has emerged as a norm in family life, in Canada as elsewhere, both within the two-parent family and emerging family structures, and after parental separation and divorce. Yet, for a significant number of children whose divorcing parents are in dispute over child caregiving arrangements, this option is essentially denied within the family court system, which continues to apply a "primary parent" and "primary residence" model. On the matter of parenting after divorce, there is a disconnection between the opinion of the Canadian judiciary and the public at large, with public opinion reflecting norms in the direction of equal and shared parental responsibility, and the judicial and legal professions the opposite. Public opinion polls indicate strong public support for shared parenting as a principle that is in the best interests of children, including in high parental conflict cases; equal parenting is supported by about 80% of the Canadian public, with a slightly higher percentage of women favouring a legal shared parenting presumption (Nanos Research 2009). Further, international law and policy are evolving beyond adversarial systems of child custody determination and primary residence orders toward the alternative of an equal or shared parenting model. As Braver et al (2011) point out, the law walks a dangerous line when it deviates from the emerging community consensus that the winner-take-all sole custody system is not working to the benefit of children and families, and that an alternative approach is urgently needed.

In accordance with public opinion, a scientific consensus has also emerged within the divorce research community in regard to the need for a humane alternative to the adversarial "sole custody" approach. The sole custody or "primary residence" model of child custody determination is not empirically supported; sole custody is associated with both diminished parent-child relationships, leading in many cases to the disengagement of a parent from children's lives and exacerbation of conflict between parents, leading in some cases to incidents of first-time family violence. The effects of these phenomena are particularly damaging to children; disrupted parent-child relationships and heightened conflict between parents lead to emotional insecurity, and compromised physical, mental, and emotional well-being of children.

The presumption of equal parenting responsibility has emerged in recent years as the most viable and humane alternative to the sole custody approach, based on widespread public and empirical support as a more equitable standard of legal determination of parenting after divorce. As will be discussed, studies comparing child and family outcomes in sole versus shared parenting arrangements show that children and parents adjust significantly better in shared parenting arrangements, even in high conflict situations. The scientific community is also drawing conclusions regarding the amount of shared parenting time necessary to achieve child well-being and positive outcomes, with an emerging consensus that a minimum of one-third time is necessary to achieve child well-being (Neilsen 2013), with additional benefits accruing up to and including equal 50–50 parenting time (Fabricius et al 2010).

Although shared parenting and joint custody legislation has been enacted in numerous jurisdictions around the globe, a clearly articulated model or presumption of equal parental responsibility that addresses the concerns of critics of shared parenting has yet to be articulated. The aim of this book is to outline the research evidence for the institution of a rebuttable legal presumption of

equal parental responsibility, or joint physical custody of children, and to articulate such a model. For our purposes, "equal
parental responsibility" is defined as children spending equal
amounts of time in each parent's household, in contested cases.
The title of the book reflects the notion that equal parenting as a
legal presumption is a presumption in more than one sense; equal
parenting has been marginalized as a viable alternative by the
Canadian legal establishment as an outlandish proposition, an
arrogant presumption of uninformed naïfs or a conspiracy of
fathers'-rights extremists that must be strongly resisted. Thus the
37,000-member Canadian Bar Association, in response to a
recent federal Conservative private member's bill in favour of
amending the Canadian Divorce Act to institutionalize equal parenting as a legal presumption, reacted swiftly and vigorously in
opposition, demanding and receiving a retraction from Conservative Minister of Justice Robert Nicholson on the motion. In addition, an abundance of lawyer-dominated federal and provincial
task force commissions and reports on family law reform avoid
any mention of equal or shared parenting as a viable legal option,
offering little more than cosmetic changes to the language of
divorce and calling for more financial support for existing legal
programs and services. Given the mounting empirical evidence
and public condemnation of the failure of the current family
law system, the "bold new reforms" heralded by these reports
and commissions amount to little more than shuffling chairs on
the Titanic.

Although equal parenting as a legal presumption, recommended as far back as 1998 by the Joint House of Commons-
Senate Committee on Child Custody and Access as the cornerstone
of needed family law reform in Canada, has been "under wraps"
in recent years and "dares not speak its name" as an evidence-
based alternative in the legal determination of parenting after
divorce in Canada, the facts that a consensus has emerged within
the scientific community and a coalition of family-law-reform
parenting groups across Canada has formed, suggest a resurgence
of support for action toward such law reform. This book presents
arguments in support of the equal parent presumption, and

addresses counter-arguments, from a child-focused and family-strengths-based perspective.

Although the book is about law reform in the direction of an equal parenting presumption, the perspective I offer is not that of a legal scholar but of a child and family social work teacher, practitioner, and researcher specializing in the area of children's needs and interests in the divorce transition. I apply a social analytical perspective to the issues, based on a focus on children's needs and parental and social institutional responsibilities to these needs, as well as on the responsibilities of social institutions to support parents in the fulfillment of their parenting responsibilities, in an attempt to find constructive and viable solutions to the present conundrum surrounding the legal determination of parenting after divorce.

My main reason for writing this book is to support the establishment of an equal-parental-responsibility presumption utilizing a "best-interests-of-the-child-from-the-perspective-of-the-child" criterion and a "responsibility-to-needs" approach to parenting after divorce. Such a social justice approach may be viewed as a needed harm reduction measure to ensure that children's relationships with both parents are legally enshrined, and that they are protected from ongoing parental conflict and risk of violence during and after their parents' divorce.

THE EQUAL PARENT PRESUMPTION

I

Equal Parenting: Rights and Responsibilities

The subject of this book is parenting after divorce. Worldwide, one in four children experience the divorce of their parents each year (Nikolina 2012), and the rise in the number of children living through the divorce of their parents is an international phenomenon. Although the outcomes for some of these children are highly problematic, most parents are able to make sound, practical agreements about their care and residence. It is the problem-oriented pole of children and parents that is our concern.

Parenting after divorce is one of the most contentious arenas of Canadian and international law. It is not a contentious issue for the majority of parents who are able to agree on post-divorce parenting arrangements; and in most non-contested cases in Canada today, parents agree to some degree of shared parenting of their children. The traditional norm of sole maternal custody after divorce has now given way to shared parental responsibility in Canadian families. It is also not contentious in cases in which family violence and child abuse have been legally established, either by means of a criminal or child welfare hearing. There is consensus that in cases involving children who are abused, including those who witness the physical abuse of a parent, equal or shared parenting is contraindicated, as these children are in need of protection from either or both parents, and a rebuttable presumption against shared parenting is applied. Yet parenting after divorce remains contentious in cases in which there is no criminal or child protection finding, and parents are in disagreement or conflict over post-divorce parenting arrangements. The focus of this book is the determination of parenting after divorce in situations in which parents cannot agree on post-divorce parenting arrangements, and negotiation efforts have failed in this regard.

When discussing "parenting after divorce," it is first necessary to clarify what is meant by "parent," and this in itself is highly contested territory. When Canadian parliament passed its gay marriage legislation, it also passed (without debate) legislation that redefined "parent" in all Canadian legal statutes, from "natural parent" to "legal parent," thereby removing, according to some socio-legal scholars, children's right to know their genetic parents (Nathanson and Young 2012; Somerville 2006). I have chosen a definition that is reflective of the majority of existing Canadian divorced families: genetic or biological parent-child relationships. Thus, I limit the definition of "parent" to "natural parent" in this book (see Somerville [2006] for a discussion of a "presumption in favour of the natural").

I define other key terms as follows: "Divorce" is defined as parental (mother and father) separation no matter whether parents are legally married or cohabiting. "Parenting after divorce" refers to parental caregiving arrangements, defined as time devoted by parental caregivers in a child's life. "Co-parenting" is defined as the involvement of both mothers and fathers in children's lives after divorce. "Shared parenting" is defined as children spending a minimum 40% proportionate time with each parent (father and mother). "Equal parenting" is a form of shared parenting in which the time division by parental caregivers is split on an equal (50%) time basis, calculated over a pre-determined period. "Primary residence" and "primary parenting" arrangements are defined as time spent by one of the parents (the "residential" parent) with children exceeding 60% proportionate time (and less than 40% by the other "non-residential" parent). There are two types of primary residence arrangements: primary residence arrangements that involve some degree of co-parenting and those that do not. When there is no form of child contact with the "non-residential" parent, I define this arrangement as a "parent absence" (most often "father absence") situation.

The ideal of equal or shared parental responsibility has been expressed in two recent changes in the laws of several countries and states outside Canada, such as the Netherlands (Nikolina 2012): the continuation of joint parental authority in children's lives after divorce, and shared parental responsibility as the first option in the legal determination of parenting after divorce. Neither "joint parental authority" nor "shared parental responsibility" are mentioned in current recent law reform efforts in Canada.

We live in an age of shared parenting responsibility, yet for a significant number of children of divorce in Canada, shared parenting is denied. This is mostly the result of misguided and outdated socio-legal policy and law. Although parental removal from children's lives in two-parent families can occur only if a child is deemed to be in need of protection from a parent by means of a thorough child welfare investigation and subsequent judicial determination, children of divorce are routinely removed from the care of one of their parents via primary residence orders under the discretionary "best-interests-of-the-child" standard, in the absence of any protection findings. When a parent is removed from the daily lives of children of divorce, these children are victims of systemic discrimination. Children of divorce are thus discriminated against on the basis of parental status simply because their parents are in dispute over their living arrangements.

Again, in contrast with other jurisdictions, a rights-based discourse continues to dominate the field of parenting after divorce in Canada. The best-interests-of-the-child standard has historically reflected a struggle between mothers' and fathers' rights, with children's needs considered to be commensurate with either position (Mason 1994). Children have been viewed at different times as fathers' property, requiring the "tender care" of mothers, and rightfully "belonging" to the sole custody of one or the other parent. Despite lip service given to the need for "joint custody" orders, discretionary best-interests-of-the-child-based judicial decisions continue to reflect a "sole custody" presumption in the form of "primary residence" orders in contested cases. In recent years, however, with increasing scrutiny of the discretionary best-interests-of-the-child standard, a new ethic has emerged which recognizes the fact that children's needs and interests are separate from, although related to, the rights of their parents. A new "parental responsibility" discourse is gradually being introduced into legal statutes and public policy, and at the level of practice.

Unlike previous examinations of child custody and access in Canada, this book proceeds from such a "parental responsibility" perspective, which acknowledges that the best interests of the child during and after parental divorce are, essentially, a matter of recognizing and addressing children's fundamental needs during and after the divorce transition. I argue that these needs are best addressed when law and social policy support parents in the fulfillment of their parental responsibilities. Such a focus is largely absent in current Canadian socio-legal discourse; the book thus aims to shift the current rights-based legal discourse of Canadian feminist and fathers' rights groups toward a responsibility-to-needs-based framework of legal determination of parenting after divorce.

A child-focused perspective in the realm of parenting after divorce is one in which children's needs and interests are of paramount concern. Consideration of the best interests of the child from the perspective of the child is missing in current deliberations. Thus the well-being of children from their own perspective takes precedence over judicial biases and preferences, professional self-interest, gender politics, the desire of a parent to remove the other from the child's life, and the wishes of a parent who is found to be a danger to the child. A child-focused approach to the legal determination of parenting after divorce also includes a careful consideration of the issues of child abuse and family violence, as children's safety trumps all other considerations in regard to their well-being.

My aim in this book is to clarify more precisely what constitutes the best interests of children in the divorce transition, from the perspective of children themselves, when their parents are in conflict over their living arrangements. To do this I apply a critical analysis to current empirical research. There are now two dozen studies on equal and shared parenting families, and from these studies a different perspective has emerged which runs counter to a number of negative assumptions and misconceptions commonly held about these families. Three decades of divorce research have made clear the fact that children fare best in post-divorce relationships in which first, they preserve meaningful and routine relationships with both of their parents, and second, are shielded from destructive parental conflict (Kelly 2007; Wallerstein and Kelly 1980; Hetherington, Cox, and Cox 1978). These two points of scientific consensus regarding what is in children's best interests after their parents' relationship ends have been acknowledged by the majority of divorce researchers for some time. Contrary to current practice and dominant socio-legal discourse in Canada, however, the research evidence over the past decade suggests that in non-protection cases of contested parenting after divorce, children's needs and well-being are best addressed by means of equal or shared parenting (Nielsen 2012; Fabricius, Diaz and Braver 2012 Cashmore and Parkinson 2010; Kaspiew et al 2009; Melli and Brown 2008; Kruk 2008). The current sole custody framework in contested cases, according to the same research, is associated with high rates of parental disengagement, increased inter-parental conflict, and markedly diminished child well-being. Contrary to dominant socio-legal discourse and current practice, the research has also found that children are not shielded from post-divorce high conflict, violence, and abuse by means of sole custody or primary residence orders (ibid). Although equal and shared parenting are contraindicated in cases of established family violence and child abuse, research shows that inter-parental conflict increases with court-mandated sole custody, as fully half of first-time family violence incidents occur after divorce, within the winner-take-all adversarial framework (Johnson and Hotton 2003; Statistics Canada 2008). Inter-parental conflict decreases within an equal or shared parenting arrangement, as neither parent is threatened by the loss of children or their parental identity. The current framework of primary residential custody decrees in disputed custody cases, contrary to dominant discourse, exposes both parents and children to violence.

The equal parental responsibility approach to the legal determination of parenting after divorce is presented here as a viable alternative to sole custody in contested cases, and as the arrangement most compatible with the stated objectives of Canadian legislative family law reform, as outlined in the Special Joint Committee on Child Custody and Access report (Special House of Commons-Senate Committee on Child Custody and Access 1998), the Federal/Provincial/Territorial Family Law Committee report (Federal-Provincial-Territorial Family Law Committee 2002), and the Child-Centred Family Justice Strategy (Department of Justice Canada 2005): to promote meaningful relationships between children and their parents following separation and divorce, encourage parental co-operation, and reduce parental conflict and litigation. It is an evidence-based approach, empirically supported as the most viable alternative to sole custody (Fabricius et al 2010; Kaspiew et al 2009; Millar 2009; Kruk 2008). This research is reinforced by strong public support for an equal parenting presumption (Braver et al 2011; Nanos Research 2009). This book is thus a call for the establishment of a legally rebuttable equal-parental-responsibility presumption in contested parenting after divorce cases, with equal parental responsibility defined as children spending equal time with each parent after separation and divorce.

In May 1997 Minister of Justice Allan Rock proposed that a joint committee of the House of Commons and Senate make recommendations regarding child custody and access. After fifty-five hearings and more than a year of study and research, the committee made forty-eight recommendations to parliament, all with an underlying theme: the sole custody-based adversarial system, as it pertains to the majority of custody and access disputes, puts families, especially children, at risk, and shared parenting should be established in law (Special House of Commons-Senate Committee on Child Custody and Access 1998). Years later, Prime Minister Stephen Harper's 2006 election platform promised to implement a presumption of shared parental responsibility, unless determined to be not in the best interests of the child, and to promote mediation as an alternative method of conflict resolution. These were the key recommendations of the Joint Committee Report in 1998, yet meaningful parenting after divorce law reform has yet to occur.

A sole custody ideology continues to prevail in judicial decision-making, reflected in assumptions that mothers are naturally better caregivers, that fathers petitioning for sole or joint custody are manipulative or seeking to avoid child support payments, and that when parents cannot agree on post-divorce parenting arrangements, children are better off in the care of one parent only (Millar 2009). Most family law matters are resolved without court orders, as judges determine post-divorce custody in a relatively small minority of cases. Yet, the influence of these decisions goes well beyond the decisions themselves. Contested cases define legal norms; the repercussions of contested cases of parenting after divorce go well beyond the cases themselves, as they serve as a baseline for the legal determination of all cases of custody disagreements, including a significant proportion of legally uncontested cases (Kruk 1993a). Collectively they form the basis of a body of law upon which all family law clients are advised. Legal negotiations are governed by expected results in the courtroom, and the spouse who expects to be awarded child custody (and its associated child and spousal support) is the one more likely to initiate court proceedings. In Canada, mothers initiate two-thirds of divorce proceedings, and there is a clear imbalance in legal awards of child custody and primary residence to mothers (Statistics Canada 2007).

Although judges are not professionally trained in child development and family dynamics, they make legal decisions largely without the benefit of credible social science evidence. Kelly and Lamb (2000) found that decisions regarding child custody and access are most often made without reference to research on child development, although this research directly concerns the needs and best interests of children of divorce. Melton (1989) presented a startling account of how little social science knowledge trickles down into the public policies that are intended to benefit children of divorce.

The discretionary best-interests-of-the-child standard and associated winner-take-all sole custody approach to family law fall prey to a number of disadvantages, which will be detailed in the chapters following. The sole custody model is fundamentally adversarial in nature, as one parent is a clear "winner" and the other a "loser" in parental status, with the designation of a "primary" and a "secondary" parent; the focus on the competing rights of parents overshadows the responsibilities of parents and social institutions to address the needs of children; and child custody and post-divorce parenting matters are seen as a one-time dispute to be resolved rather than a long-term process that will naturally change and evolve over time. I will pose nine arguments against the discretionary best-interests-of-the-child standard. I do not propose abandoning the principle that the needs and interests of children should be the paramount consideration in parenting after divorce; rather, I argue that the "best interests of children" should be clearly defined and based on available research evidence regarding children's needs and factors associated with their well-being after divorce, and applied to children's and families' individual circumstances, rather than being based on judicial discretion. In regard to the specific flaws of the discretionary standard, I will argue as follows: the vagueness and indeterminacy of the discretionary best-interests-of-the-child standard, which gives unfettered discretion to judges not trained in child development and family dynamics, results in unpredictable and inconsistent outcomes based on idiosyncratic biases and subjective value-based judgments; the discretionary best-interests-of-the-child standard is subject to judicial error, leading to potentially harmful outcomes; discretionary best-interests-of-the-child-based decisions reflect a sole custody presumption; the discretionary best-interests-of-the-child standard sustains, intensifies and creates conflict, and fuels litigation; the discretionary best-interests-of-the-child standard makes the court dependent on professional evaluations of parenting after divorce which lack an empirical foundation; the views of children and parents regarding the best interests of the child are very different to those of the judiciary; the current best-interests-of-the-child standard is a smokescreen for the underlying issue of the judiciary and legal system retaining their decision-making power in the parenting after divorce realm; within the present system, children of divorce are discriminated against on the basis of parental status in regard to the removal of their parents from their lives; and, despite best-interests rhetoric, the parties in the legal proceedings are parents whose legal counsel represents their interests, not those of their children, and children's true needs are lost within a forum where the parties equate their children's needs with their own interests.

The book will also provide an in-depth discussion of sixteen arguments for an equal-parental-responsibility presumption, as follows: equal parenting preserves children's relationships with both parents; equal parenting preserves parents' relationships with their children; equal parenting decreases parental conflict and prevents family violence; equal parenting reflects children's preferences and views about their needs and best interests; equal parenting reflects parents' preferences and views about their children's needs and best interests; equal parenting reflects child caregiving arrangements before divorce; equal parenting enhances the quality of parent-child relationships; equal parenting decreases parental focus on "mathematizing time" and reduces litigation; equal parenting provides an incentive for inter-parental negotiation, mediation, and the development of parenting plans; equal parenting provides a clear and consistent guideline for judicial decision-making; equal parenting reduces the risk and incidence of parental alienation; equal parenting enables enforcement of parenting orders, as parents are more likely to abide by an equal parenting order; equal parenting addresses social justice imperatives regarding protection of children's rights; equal parenting addresses social justice imperatives regarding parental authority, autonomy, equality, rights, and responsibilities; the discretionary best-interests-of-the-child/sole custody model is not empirically supported; and, a rebuttable legal presumption of equal parenting responsibility is empirically supported.

The exponential growth of the child custody industry and professional self-interest, together with the power- and ownership-based ideology of child custody, have prevailed over children's needs for the active and responsible involvement of both parents in their lives and to be shielded from ongoing parental conflict and family violence. The state has disengaged from its responsibility to support parents in the fulfillment of their parental obligations. In particular, often overlooked by professional service providers and policymakers are the devastating effects of parental disengagement, especially father absence, on children's lives, and the corresponding effects of child absence on parents alienated from their children's lives. The removal of parents from children's lives following divorce is but one manifestation of the general disappearance of parents from children's lives, the direct result of current child and family policies, including child care, child protection, and child custody policies which undermine rather than support parents in the fulfillment of their parental responsibilities.

The book's main contribution is the provision of a template for equal parenting legislation, based on a child-focused best-interests-of-the-child-from-the-perspective-of-the-child legal standard, and a responsibility-to-needs approach to the legal determination of parenting after divorce. The equal parenting presumption, comprised of four pillars of legal determination of parenting after divorce, is evidence-based in its consideration of the implications of child-focused empirical research on children's needs and well-being in the divorce transition, and on research on child and family outcomes in jurisdictions around the world that have enacted some form of shared parenting legislation. The four-pillar approach discussed here, however, goes beyond what other jurisdictions have attempted in shared parenting law, toward a more social-justice-based model of equal parenting. The four-pillar approach encompasses the following components: (1) a rebuttable legal presumption of equal parenting responsibility in family law, based on a best-interests-of-the-child-from-the-perspective-of-the-child standard and a responsibility-to-needs approach; (2) treatment comprised of universal access to divorce education, mediation, and specialized support services in high conflict cases; (3) prevention in the form of equal parenting public education; and (4) enforcement focused on both parenting orders and judicial determination of parenting arrangements in cases of established abuse and family violence. Within the first pillar (the best-interests-of-the-child-from-the-perspective-of-the-child standard and a responsibility-to-needs approach), discussion of the equal-parenting-responsibility presumption will focus on four key elements: (1) a "parenting plan" requirement for all parents in dispute over matters related to parenting after divorce; (2) the application of an "approximation standard" for parents who cannot agree on a parenting plan, in which existing parent-child relationships would continue after divorce; (3) the implementation of equal parenting time for parents who were both primary caregivers before divorce; and (4) a presumption against equal parenting responsibility when it has been legally established that a child is in need of protection from a parent or parents. Within the treatment pillar, a detailed framework for divorce education and therapeutic family mediation for high conflict parents will be outlined.

About This Book

A best-interests-of-the-child-from-the-perspective-of-the-child legal standard and parental-responsibility-to-children's-needs framework for the legal determination of parenting after divorce has yet to be undertaken. This is the principal aim of this book, which will first provide a critical overview of divorce research from a child-focused perspective, and then seek to clearly define children's best interests in terms of their essential needs in the separation and divorce transition, enumerate parental responsibilities vis-à-vis these needs, and outline the responsibilities of social institutions such as the courts and legislatures to support parents in the fulfillment of their parental obligations. I will then state the case for a rebuttable legal presumption of equal parental responsibility or joint physical custody of children in contested parenting after divorce cases, including a critical analysis of the discretionary best-interests-of-the-child standard and an overview of the principal arguments in favour of equal parenting. Finally, I will outline in detail the equal parenting presumption, comprised of four pillars of legal determination of parenting after divorce: legal presumption of equal parental responsibility, treatment, prevention, and enforcement.

The book is organized as follows: Chapter 2 will examine the current state of parenting after divorce legislation and practice in Canada and abroad; despite claims that shared parenting and joint custody are being increasingly ordered in contested cases, an examination of child outcomes will reveal how "joint custody" exists in name only, as courts rarely deviate from the imposition of "primary residence" orders. Chapter 3 focuses on new directions in divorce and child custody law and practice in Canada and abroad; again, despite strong empirical and public support for equal parenting, opposition from bar associations and the judiciary has curtailed the development of equal parenting legislation, even in jurisdictions like Australia that have attempted to institutionalize shared parenting law. Chapter 4 examines the flaws of the discretionary best-interests-of-the-child principle and details the harms associated with the winner-take-all adversarial approach to the legal determination of parenting after divorce. Chapter 5 presents an overview of current research on children's needs and interests in the divorce transition, with a focus on key research findings over the past decade. The link between children's well-being and their meaningful involvement with both parents after divorce is discussed. Chapter 6 focuses on the second key factor in children's adjustment to the consequences of divorce: the importance of shielding children from ongoing high conflict and family violence. In chapter 7, I present the case in support of equal parenting as an alternative to the sole custody approach to the legal determination of parenting after divorce, and of the equal parenting presumption as an alternative to the discretionary best-interests-of-the-child standard. Sixteen arguments in support of the presumption will be presented, and counter-arguments addressed, from a child-focused perspective, and clinical and empirical evidence in support of each argument will be contrasted with the conflicting evidence. Chapter 8 outlines the equal parenting presumption in detail, including its four pillars and its equal-parental-responsibility approach. This chapter thus provides a template for the institutionalization of the equal parenting presumption by state legislatures. I conclude with a consideration of special challenges and specific recommendations vis-à-vis equal parenting in chapters 9 and 10.

In sum, the book is dedicated to the principle of social justice for children of divorce. First, I will examine the principle from children's own perspective: shifting the best-interests concept and the determination of parenting after divorce away from the application of a discretionary standard toward a more child-focused approach, one based on the best-interests-of-the-child-from-the-perspective-of-the-child. Second, I extend the definition of social justice for children of divorce beyond a children's-rights-based notion toward a responsibility-to-needs framework in which parents are better supported by state institutions in the fulfillment of their parental responsibilities vis-à-vis their children's needs. Although children's rights are discussed in some detail, including the right of active, meaningful, and responsible involvement of both parents in their lives, and the right to not be discriminated against on the basis of parental status in regard to the removal of one of their parents from their lives, too much emphasis on rights diverts attention away from a more fundamental aspect of social justice for children, that of responsibilities. Children's needs during and after the divorce transition, parental responsibilities to those needs, and the responsibilities of social institutions to support parents in the exercise of their parental responsibilities constitute the foundation of social justice for children of divorce, and the foundation for this book.

2

Parenting after Divorce:
Federal and International Law

FEDERAL AND PROVINCIAL / TERRITORIAL
LEGISLATION IN CANADA

Family law in Canada is a complex overlay of statute law, common law, case law, and constitutional law. In Canada as elsewhere, the demise of the maternal presumption and its replacement by the principle that child custody ought to be decided according to what is in the best interests of the child occurred in the 1970s. In Canada, the maternal preference rule remained in place until the formal introduction of the best-interests-of-the-child standard via Canada's current Divorce Act (1986), whose wording reflects a careful consideration for gender neutrality. Paradoxically, the new act coincided with a proportionally larger share of judicial determinations of sole maternal residence. Since 1986, a major expansion of family law has occurred, with considerable reliance on parental gender as a key factor in custody decisions, in the absence of precisely defined predictors of the best interests of the child (Millar 2009).

As Mason (1994) notes, despite the promise of gender neutrality and the claim that the court may consider the interests only of children in best-interests-of-the-child custody cases, children's best interests have historically been equated with the interests of one or the other of their parents, and this pattern continues to the present day, as evidenced by maternal custody outcomes and primary residence decrees in the great majority of contested cases (Millar 2009). And as Canadian family law is based on the English common law tradition, which derives law from both written statutes and from common law, also known as case law, precedent law, or judge-made law, judges make new rules for new situations as they arise. Due to the general indeterminacy of language, and often to the deliberately vague drafting of statutes by legislators, there is no absolute distinction between common law and statute law. The application of the law in any given area may be either statute-like or common-law-like, depending on the scope allowed for judicial discretion due to the indeterminacy of the statutory language. The more vague and indeterminate statutes are, the more judges must use their own experience and intellect to interpret and apply them in particular cases, to give concrete meaning to the statutes. Needed interpretation of statutes by judges gives rise to case law, which formulates precedents usually involving presumptions or guiding principles for future cases of a similar nature. Case law gives rise to the interpretation of statutes and the formulation of precedents. Judges cannot interpret statutes of their own accord.

Although Canadian child custody law derives from both legislation and precedent, given the indeterminacy of family law, precedent is the stronger of the two. In this way, Canada has maintained a maternal custody preference throughout most of its history, as the legal environment relating to parenting after divorce has been mainly shaped and controlled through judge-made law, legal concepts, and presumptions developed though precedent.

Legislative responsibility for parenting after divorce in Canada is shared among the federal, provincial, and territorial governments. The federal Divorce Act (Government of Canada 1985) applies in divorce proceedings when child custody issues arise, although they may be resolved under provincial legislation. Provincial and territorial statutes govern cases of parents who are legally not married, which fall within provincial constitutional responsibility, including parental separation proceedings involving disputes over parenting after divorce.

The following is a brief overview of federal and provincial statutes respecting parenting after divorce, and child custody and access. Provincial legislatures have had to draft legislation concerning the best interests of the child to fill the gaping holes of the Divorce Act (Government of Canada 1985), by passing statutes that deal with the considerations judges must take into account when making a discretionary determination of the best interests of the child.

Federal Legislation

Federal divorce legislation in Canada holds the best interests of the child as the paramount criterion in determining post-divorce parenting arrangements, trumping even constitutional provisions. The Divorce Act uses the terms "custody" and "access" to describe post-divorce parenting arrangements. "Custody" includes "care, upbringing, and any other incident of custody" (Section 2 (1)). "Access" is not specifically defined. Either or both spouses, or any other person, may apply for custody of, or access to, a child. The Divorce Act permits the court to make interim and final (sole or joint) custody and access orders and enables it to impose terms, conditions, and restrictions in connection with those orders.

Section 16 (8) of the Divorce Act states: "the court shall take into consideration only the best interests of the child of the marriage as determined by reference to the condition, means, needs, and other circumstances of the child." Section 16 (10) reads: "the child of the marriage should have as much contact with each spouse as is consistent with the best interests of the child and, for that purpose, shall take into consideration the willingness of the person for whom custody is sought to facilitate such contact" (the so-called "friendly parent" rule).

Although the Divorce Act identifies "the best interests of the child" as the sole criterion in the legal determination of parenting after divorce, it identifies neither the specific "needs and other circumstances of the child" that must be considered in determining custodial arrangements, nor the specific criteria used to determine the best interests of children, and thus the standard remains indeterminate and subject to judicial discretion. In addition, no mention is made of the primacy of both parents in the child's life. In Canada, parents have no constitutional protection for their parenting rights; the courts are the "ultimate legal parents" of all children in Canada, and parental rights can be revoked any time the judiciary chooses. As will be discussed in chapter 4, legal determination of parenting after divorce in Canada is not so much a decision to award custody, but a decision regarding from whom to remove it.

Provincial/Territorial Legislation

Provincial and territorial child and family legislation relevant to parenting after divorce, child custody, and access includes the British Columbia Family Law Act, 2011 (Sections 40–43), Alberta Family Law Act 2003 (Sections 32 and 35), Saskatchewan Children's Law Act 1997 (Sections 8 and 9), Manitoba Family Maintenance Act 2012 (Section 39), Ontario Children's Law Reform Act 1990 (Sections 20–27), Quebec Civil Code of Procedure 2013 (Articles 597–612), New Brunswick Family Services Act 1980 (Sections 111–137), Nova Scotia Maintenance and Custody Act 1989 (Section 18), Prince Edward Island Family Law Act and Custody Jurisdiction and Enforcement Act 1988 (Sections 3–6), Newfoundland and Labrador Children's Law Act 1990 (Sections 24–54), Yukon Family Property and Support Act 2002 (Sections 64), Northwest Territories Children's Law Act 1997 (Section 18), and Nunavut Children's Law Act 1997 (Section 18). All cite the best interests of the child as the sole criterion in the legal determination of parenting after divorce, yet they provide minimal indicators of these best interests, and, when still used, neither "custody" nor "access" are clearly defined. There is also substantial heterogeneity in the factors that provincial and territorial statutes identify as relevant to a child's best interests.

CASE LAW / OUTCOMES OF LITIGATED CASES

Whereas few jurisdictions globally have a legal presumption that a court must order the physical care of a child to one parent over the other in legally contested cases, research indicates that de facto sole custody/primary residence arrangements continue to prevail. Some of these are due to the fact that one parent walks away from his/her responsibilities; others are due to family court constraints. As the latter is a preventable measure with more enlightened legislation, it is our focus here.

Courts in all Canadian provinces and territories continue to make legal determinations that "award" primary rights to and responsibilities for children to one parent in the majority of cases, despite the fact that when both parents reside together, legal "custody" is held equally by both of them. Primary residence orders that place children in the residence of one parent, and provide "contact" with the other, constitute the normal court practice across Canada in disputed cases, although these arrangements are often designated "joint custody." Decision-making in these cases is legally shared, whereas residence is not; some have argued that decisions made by parents regarding children are and need to be made in the course of daily life, routines, and residence.

According to data on court orders from the Central Registry of Divorce Proceedings, primary residence was awarded to mothers in 49.5% of cases, joint custody to both parents in 41.8% of cases, and father residence in only 8.5% of cases (Statistics Canada 2007). The decree of "joint custody," however, is typically made with a primary residence provision, meaning that children primarily reside with one parent. Joint decision-making without physical shared custody is awarded. Further, to say "joint custody was awarded" in 41.8% of cases is somewhat misleading, as this statistic includes "judge-ratified," non-contested custody cases (those shared parenting decisions made by parents themselves and "rubber-stamped" by a judge). This statistic comprises all "custody arrangements that were part of the divorce judgment," which includes the majority of cases which are ratifications of parental agreements; these are not all litigated cases of child custody. Shared parenting in litigated cases, particularly those involving high conflict, is deemed by the judiciary to be unworkable.

As it is the litigated cases that are of most interest to policy-makers and researchers, Millar (2009) analyzed the Statistics

Canada Central Divorce Registry (CDR) dataset from the proclamation of the current Divorce Act on June 1, 1986, to September 30, 2002, to isolate the impact of the gender of the parent as a predictor of custody awards, examining de facto living arrangements specified by judges. The CDR dataset yielded over 1.1 million parent-child pairings. The mother obtained either sole custody or joint custody with primary residence in 89% of these pairs. The dataset also contains information about the circumstances of the divorce, including which party initiated the action, the grounds pled, whether or not there was a hearing to determine custody, family size, age and position of the child within the family, age of each of the parents, region of the country, year of the divorce, and duration of the marriage. Millar completed a multinomial regression that found that mothers were more than twenty-seven times as likely as fathers to obtain sole custody.

In non-contested child custody cases, in which parents themselves determined child custody arrangements, a marked decrease in sole maternal outcomes and increase in both shared and equal parenting outcomes has been noted (Statistics Canada 2007). Equal and shared parenting has been steadily increasing in non-litigated cases in Canada, which reflects the emerging norm of shared parental responsibility in two-parent families.

National Longitudinal Survey of Children and Youth

The National Longitudinal Survey of Children and Youth (NLSCY), which tracks a large sample of Canadian children as they grow up, utilizes data from the parent deemed the "person most knowledgeable" about the child (which excludes parents with equal parenting arrangements) and, more than 90% of the time, this person was a woman, and, in most cases, the mother of the child. However, as mothers' and fathers' perceptions of child custody differ markedly (LeBourdais, Juby, and Marcil-Gratton 2001), this data set is far from complete. Nevertheless, NLSCY data track both married and co-habiting couples, as the proportion of children born to co-habiting couples in Canada is now 22% (Juby, Marcil-Gratton, and LeBourdais 2004). Data reveal that by the age of fifteen, 30% of Canadian children born to a couple in the early 1980s had experienced their parents' divorce, and that equal and shared parenting is much more frequent in this demographic when the divorce was settled outside the court. The NLSCY found that the proportion of children in non-litigated, post-divorce, joint custody arrangements has increased markedly (ibid), confirming Statistics Canada (2007) data which indicates that sole maternal custody no longer comprises the majority of post-divorce living arrangements in Canada.

Millar (2009) analyzed the NLSCY dataset to identify the variables that correlate with positive and negative outcomes for children of divorce, with particular attention to parenting attributes. He found that assignment of sole parenting to mothers was associated with increases in emotional disorders in children, while assignment of sole parenting to fathers was associated with increases in hyperactivity and behavioural problems.

Impact of Contested Cases

Equal or shared parenting (or joint residence) orders are very rarely ordered in judge-adjudicated cases in Canada; in the vast majority of contested or litigated cases over the past twenty years, primary residence awards have been made to mothers (Millar 2009). It has been argued, however, that only a small percentage of cases reach trial over the issue, and thus it is the family and not the court that determines who will have responsibility for the parenting of the children in the majority of cases; it is argued that the court simply ratifies existing arrangements made by the parties. Thus Polikoff (1982, 183) points out that most children remain with their mothers by the mutual consent of the parents: "The final court award, rubber stamping the arrangement of the parties themselves, does not reflect a bias on the part of the court system toward mothers because the court system plays an entirely passive role." However, although less than 5% of divorces involving dependent children come to trial over the issue of parenting after divorce, data on outcomes in family court suggest that many "parental agreements," made in the shadow of contested cases at trial, may be much more contentious than is assumed. Contested case outcomes are instructive inasmuch as they inform how lawyers will advise their clients in potential child custody cases. A scrutiny of contested cases of child custody in Canada provides an explanation for the relatively low levels of legally disputed cases. The impact of judicial decisions in contested cases goes well beyond the cases themselves. They define legal norms and form the basis of a body of law upon which others are advised, including the bulk of "uncontested" cases in which fathers want at least shared parenting but "settle" for access or visitation (Kruk 1993a). "Bargaining in the shadow of the law" refers to legal negotiations framed and shaped by the perception of the parties of what results might be achieved if they resorted to greater legal involvement. Although the majority of primary residence court orders are "consent" orders (and included by Statistics Canada as court determinations), this should not imply that these orders are entered into freely (Millar and Goldenberg 2004).

INTERNATIONAL LAW BY WHICH CANADA IS BOUND

Children's rights related to their relationship with their parents have a long history in international law, starting with the International Covenant on Civil and Political Rights (ICCPR) in 1976 (acceded to by Canada on May 19, 1976 and entered into force for Canada on August 19, 1976, see: treaties.un.org). This treaty includes provisions obliging member states to protect the family and children (Sections 23 and 24 respectively) and to make provisions to protect children in case of the dissolution of their parents' marriage (Section 23(4)). According to Section 24, the protection of children and the family encompasses the bond between children and both parents, which needs to be protected and maintained, regardless of whether the parents themselves are still living together. The minimal means of achieving this goal is to ensure contact (access) between the parents and child, but shared parenting is preferred, as Section 23(4) refers to the equality of the parents in regard to the right to regular contact with their children. The ICCPR prescribes that "any discriminatory treatment regarding child custody must be prohibited."

Canada acceded to the mirror-treaty of the ICCPR, the International Covenant on Economic, Social, and Cultural Rights (ICESCR), on the same date. The provisions held in this treaty are of an economic, social, and cultural nature and therefore are more difficult to both define and uphold in practice. Section 10 provides that the widest possible protection and assistance should be accorded to the family, and that children should not be discriminated against for reasons of parentage or other conditions. Central to the definition of "family" here is the parent-child relationship. Thus, the ICESCR adds economic, social, and cultural protection to the political and legal protection granted by the ICCPR. Economic protection of the parent-child bond would, for example, entail financial help to support parents in their responsibilities, and to maintain the relationship between parents and their children.

A more recent and likely the most influential international UN treaty in the field of family law is the Convention on the Rights of the Child (CRC), which entered into force for Canada on January 12, 1992. Unlike the ICCPR, this treaty is fully focused on children's rights and devotes significant attention to the parent-child relationship. This treaty establishes a right to know and be cared for by one's parents (Article 7). This right, together with the right not to be separated from one's parent (Article 9) was originally focused on preventing States Parties from unlawfully interfering in family relations, but has since established rules on dealing with the parent-child relationship, which come down to the following: when deciding if a child should be separated from one or both of his or her parents against a parent's wishes, the child's best interests should be a primary consideration and all interested parties, including the child in question if the child is mature enough, should be given an opportunity to participate in the proceedings and make their views known (see Articles 3, 9, and 12). This could indicate that once both parents have custody or parental responsibility over their child, it should not be taken away, unless to do so would be in the best interests of the child.

Article 9 (3) becomes applicable after parental divorce, and grants the child the right to maintain personal relations and direct contact with both parents on a regular basis, unless this is contrary to the child's best interests. Finally, Article 2 stipulates that States Parties must ensure that children's rights are respected without discrimination of any kind, including discrimination based on parental status.

Although the CRC does not explain what kind of actions should be considered to be in the best of the child, the notion itself permeates the treaty. It can either be used as grounds for departure from other rights in the treaty, as an addition to these rights, or as a stand-alone principle. Nevertheless, the Convention emphasizes that the primary responsibility for the upbringing and development of children falls on both parents. States Parties must respect the responsibilities, rights and duties of the parents (Article 5), and must render assistance to parents in the performance of their child-rearing responsibilities (Article 18).

Recent Developments in International Law

Canada is a member of the Hague Conference on Private International Law (www.hcch.net) and has ratified or acceded to many of its conventions, including the Convention of October 25, 1980 on the Civil Aspects of International Child Abduction and the Convention of May 29, 1993 on Protection of Children and Co-operation in Respect of Intercountry Adoption. The Hague Conference drafts conventions that deal with problems that are not confined to the territory of a single country. They usually specify which judge has jurisdiction and which national law is applicable to the dispute, along with other procedural questions. This promotes legal transparency and ensures that cases do not fall between jurisdictions.

Apart from the two above-mentioned conventions, there is another Hague convention that deals with all issues concerning the protection of children, but the latter has not been ratified by Canada. While the Child Abduction Convention and the Intercountry Adoption Convention deal with specific issues, the

1996 Convention on jurisdiction, applicable law, recognition, enforcement, and co-operation in respect of parental responsibilities and measures for the protection of children is an overarching, general convention that provides guidance in disputes concerning children, including issues of child custody and parental responsibility. The Convention states in in its preamble that the best interests of the child should be a primary consideration. Hearing the child is also seen as very important. Not providing an opportunity for the child to be heard is in fact a valid reason to not recognize a foreign measure (Section 23(2)(b)). The Convention has been ratified by forty-two countries and signed by an additional five, including the United States, but not Canada.

Developments in European Law

In Europe, there are two major organizations that draft (binding and non-binding) legal instruments: the Council of Europe and the European Union (EU). The EU has become more active in the field of family law, its legislation mostly focused on the protection of the right of the child to have direct contact with both of his or her parents (Section 24(3) of the Charter on Fundamental Rights of the European Union) and setting down procedural rules in cross-border family law cases in, for example, the Rome III and the Brussels II Regulations.

The Council of Europe is the organisation behind the Convention for the Protection of Human Rights and Fundamental Freedoms (ECHR). This is a binding, European human rights instrument, enacted in 1950, which, over the years, has generated a vast amount of case law. The Convention protects the right to family life and prohibits discrimination in cases in which post-divorce disputes over child custody are involved (Articles 8 and 14), which implies the following: a parent and child share a natural bond, which falls within the definition of family life, and needs to be protected from interference by the state. The parents are equal before the law and should not be discriminated against, for example, on the basis of gender. In a case from 2009, it was decided that where harmonious shared residence and shared care exists before parental divorce, joint custody should be granted after divorce upon request, even against the wishes of one of the parents (Zaunegger v. Germany, Application No. 22028/04, December 3, 2009).

The Council of Europe has adopted two conventions concerning children aside from the ECHR: the European Convention on the Exercise of Children's Rights, and the Convention on Contact Concerning Children. Only a small number of countries have ratified these conventions (sixteen and six, respectively). The non-binding Recommendation on Parental Responsibilities was adopted by the Council of Europe in 1984. While recommendations do not legally bind the member states, they have a strong persuasive effect, as they were drafted by renowned national experts and based on empirical research. The Recommendation sets out how parental responsibilities and child custody should be allocated in different situations, when the competent authority should take measures if parental responsibilities are misused, and what some of the responsibilities entail. It takes a reserved approach to shared parental responsibility after divorce: the national competent authority should provide that parental responsibilities should be exercised jointly only if both parents consent.

Starting in 1997, attempts have been made to update the principles laid down in the 1984 Recommendation. Originally, it was intended to become a new binding instrument, but the form of a recommendation was chosen instead. A White Paper was written in 2002, which strongly promoted shared parental responsibility and legal joint custody, and created a favourable framework for equal parenting. Not much was done with it until 2010, when the Draft Recommendation on the Rights and Legal Status of Children and Parental Responsibilities was completed.

This Draft Recommendation has a strong presumption of shared parental responsibility (legal joint custody) as it should in principle belong to each parent, and the dissolution, termination, or annulment of the parents' marriage or other formal relationship, or their legal or factual separation, should not as such constitute a reason for terminating parental responsibilities, by operation of law (Section 23). If a parent does not hold parental responsibilities, he or she should be able to acquire them, unless this is against the child's best interests, which would be rare, as shared parental responsibility is considered to generally be in the child's best interests. The lack of consent of a parent as an obstacle for gaining shared parental responsibility has disappeared from the text of the Draft Recommendation. Shared physical care of the child is seen as the preferable model to exercise shared parental responsibility.

International law provides an international legal framework within which Canadian laws have to function. As will become clear, Canadian statutes and practices fall far short of international law provisions respecting the needs and interests of children of divorce, particularly in regard to shared parental responsibility of children after divorce.

3

New Developments in National and International Socio-legal Policy

FEDERAL AND PROVINCIAL REPORTS ON FAMILY LAW REFORM

The plethora of Canadian government policy and research papers and reports on parenting after divorce, as well as provincial government papers, have for the most part neither sought to delineate specific indicators related to the best-interests-of-the-child standard of judicial decision-making, nor addressed the issue of gender stratification in sole custody/primary residence decisions in contested cases. Federal and provincial/territorial reports on family law reform do, however, expressly endorse the need for judicial discretion in the determination of the best interests of the child and post-divorce parenting arrangements in contested cases. The *Federal-Provincial-Territorial Report on Child Custody and Access and Child Support* (2002, 18) recommends that "legislation not establish any presumptive model of parenting after separation, nor contain any language that suggests a presumptive model." The new British Columbia Family Law Act (2011) also makes no mention of alternatives to the discretionary best-interests-of-the-child approach, including equal or shared parental responsibility. Government reports, both federal and provincial, and provincial law reform efforts, call for largely cosmetic changes, such as changing legal terminology and the language of family law statutes, with "custody" being replaced by "guardianship," and "access" by "parenting time." Although the Act recognizes common-law relationships and same-sex marriage, outlines procedures to determine parentage in situations in which new reproductive technologies and surrogacy are used, and creates a family arbitration process via parenting coordination in contested cases – all important advances in divorce legislation – problems affecting the bulk of divorce impasses in which parenting after divorce is at issue are left unaddressed.

Much of the focus of government reports and law reform efforts respecting parenting after divorce has been on the need for more judges, additional training for judges in family law matters, and the expansion of support services for parents. Above all else, the retention of judicial discretion regarding the best-interests-of-the-child standard, and not disturbing the present practice of de facto sole custody/primary residence orders in contested cases is emphasized. Given the views of legal commentators who argue that the indeterminacy of the best-interests-of-the-child criterion is highly problematic in child custody proceedings (Bala 2000; Elster 1987), it is legitimate to question why a matter as important as the best interests of children remains subject to judicial discretion.

Special Joint Committee Report

Numerous federal government reports on parenting after divorce, child custody, and access have been commissioned over the past twenty years, few of which have attempted to clarify or refine the best-interests criterion. The most comprehensive research-based report to date, however, is a notable exception. The Special House of Commons Senate Joint Committee on Child Custody and Access report, *For the Sake of the Children* (1998), more than any previous examination, sought to assess current research and its implications for parenting after divorce, child custody and access in Canada. This report, unlike others before and since, focused on shared parenting, parent education and mediation, and defining children's needs and paternal responsibilities in the divorce transition based on the UN Convention on the Rights of the Child. It thus remains a benchmark report in regard to examining the core issues related to parenting after divorce, and, not surprisingly, it goes well beyond the cosmetic changes recommended by other reports.

Many briefs to the Joint Committee, from legal practitioners, mental health specialists, parents' groups, and children's representatives, stressed that a new divorce act should affirm that both parents should be responsible for the daily care of their children after divorce, as reflected in the Committee's statement that, "parents' relationships with their children do not end upon separation or divorce ... Divorced parents and their children are entitled to a close and continuous relationship with one another" (Special Joint House of Commons-Senate Committee on Child Custody and Access 1998, 11). The main recommendation of the Joint Committee was that a shared parenting approach should replace traditional sole custody and access determinations. The Committee further recommended the use of "parenting plans," developed according to the best interests of the children, "setting out details about each parent's responsibilities for residence, care, decision-making, and financial security for the children ... All parenting orders should be in the form of parenting plans" (ibid, 12). The issue of family violence was a primary focus of the Joint Committee's deliberations, and its main recommendation in regard to family violence highlighted the need for non-adversarial means of dispute resolution, including parent education programs and the requirement that parents "attend at least one mediation session to help them develop a parenting plan for their children" (ibid, 12).

The Joint Committee concluded that the current Divorce Act requires revision in a number of key areas. A new act, according to the Committee, should assume the existence of two parenting households and reflect that shared parental responsibility is in children's best interests. It should also take into account the importance of grandparents, siblings, and other extended family members in children's lives. Family mediation should exist alongside rather than replace the legal system. Attending at least one confidential mediation session should be mandatory; indeed, the Committee stressed that the law should affirm that mediation and other methods of dispute resolution be the first choice in cases of marital breakdown.

It was noted by the Committee that for its recommendations to be properly realized, federal and provincial governments must commit adequate resources to develop comprehensive parent education programs, offer therapeutic family mediation, and identify in law specific criteria related to the best interests of the child, particularly in regard to the continued involvement of both parents in children's lives. Finally, lawyers, judges, and mediators should see themselves as parts of a single team, working together to help divorcing parents formulate workable and effective shared parenting plans.

Response to the Special Joint Committee Report

In response to the Special Joint Committee report *For the Sake of the Children*, the Federal-Provincial-Territorial Family Law Committee set out a list of guiding principles for the reform of child custody and access law in a 2002 report, *Putting Children First*. This report, inasmuch as it focused on the essential needs of children in the divorce transition, established guidelines for the development of a new approach to the legal determination of parenting after divorce, as follows: (1) ensure that the needs and well-being of children are primary; (2) promote parenting arrangements that foster and encourage continued parenting responsibilities by both parents, when it is safe to do so; (3) provide clarity in the law with respect to specific factors of what is in the best interests of the child; (4) promote alternative dispute resolution mechanisms to allow conflicts to be resolved in a non-adversarial forum and co-operative fashion; (5) ensure that conflicts are resolved in an accessible, fair, and timely manner; and (6) encourage the participation of extended family and grandparents in the child's life, when it is safe to do so.

Also, in 2002, Justice Canada embarked on the implementation of its Child-Centred Family Justice Strategy. The purpose of the strategy was to help parents focus on the needs of their children following separation and divorce. It was composed of three pillars: family justice services, legislative reform, and the expansion of Unified Family Courts. The strategy proposed that the best-interests-of-the-child principle be reaffirmed and strengthened by adding a list of best-interests criteria to the Divorce Act, as follows:

- the child's physical, emotional, and psychological needs, including the child's need for stability, taking into account the child's age and stage of development;
- the benefit to the child of developing and maintaining meaningful relationships with both parents and each parent's willingness to support the development and maintenance of the child's relationship with the other parent;
- the history of care for the child;
- any family violence, including its impact on the safety of the child and other family members, the child's general well-being, the ability of the person who engaged in the family violence to care for and meet the needs of the child, and the appropriateness of making an order that would require the parents to co-operate on issues affecting the child;
- the child's cultural, linguistic, religious, and spiritual upbringing and heritage, including aboriginal upbringing or heritage;
- the child's views and preferences to the extent that those can be reasonably ascertained;
- any plans proposed for the child's care and upbringing;
- the nature, strength, and stability of the relationship between the child and each parent;
- the nature, strength, and stability of the relationship between the child and each sibling, grandparent, and any other significant person in the child's life;
- the ability of each person in respect of whom the order would apply to care for and meet the needs of the child;
- the ability of each person in respect of whom the order would apply to communicate and co-operate on issues affecting the child; and
- any court order or criminal conviction that is relevant to the safety or well-being of the child.

This proposed reform is based on a parental responsibility model, and its underlying concept is that both parents will be responsible for the well-being of their children after divorce. Parents should carry out their obligations to their children largely at their own discretion, using the best-interests criteria as a guide. The parenting arrangements they make will include allocating parenting time based on a residential schedule that sets out the time that children spend with each parent, and decision-making responsibilities regarding children's health, education, and religious upbringing. When a judge is needed to make a decision, the judge will issue a "parenting order" allocating parental responsibilities.

Taking the guiding principles of the Federal-Provincial-Territorial Family Law Committee as well as the guidelines of the Child-Centred Family Justice Strategy as the foundation for legislative reform, Bill C-22, Reform of the Divorce Act Respecting Child Custody and Access, was introduced by Jean Chretien's Liberal government, but subsequently shelved by Stephen Harper's Conservative government. Essentially, Bill C-22 endorsed a "parental responsibility model" in which the terms "custody" and "access" would be eliminated and "parental responsibility" introduced, to allow courts to allocate child care-giving responsibilities between the parents. The law would encourage regular interaction between children and both parents, but would not require that parenting responsibilities be divided on a shared or equal basis between parents. The best interests of the child would still be subject to judicial discretion.

A legal presumption of shared parenting after separation and divorce is one of the stated aims of the ruling Conservative Party's policies on parenting after divorce. The Conservatives' stated position during the 2006 federal election was the implementation of the Special Joint Committee's recommendation that the rights and responsibilities of child-rearing be shared between the parents, unless demonstrated not to be in the best interests of the child. The terms "custody" and "access" would be removed from the law and replaced with "shared parenting." The "parenting plan" approach recommended by the Joint Committee would be used to allocate parental responsibilities, and a shared parenting presumption in disputed cases, unless not in the best interests of the child, would be legislated.

In June 2009, a Conservative member of parliament, Maurice Vellacott, introduced a private-member's bill, Bill C-422, calling for the legal presumption of shared parenting after divorce in cases not involving family violence or abuse. This bill was a topic of concern at the August 2009 annual conference of the Canadian Bar Association. At the conference, the federal justice minister, Robert Nicholson, when pressed, announced his opposition to the bill, stating that the discretionary best-interests-of-the-child standard should and would remain as the foundation of the legal determination of parenting after divorce in Canada, in direct contradiction to the official position of the Conservative Party during the previous federal election.

INTERNATIONAL LAW AND POLICY

Whereas action on family law reform in Canada has not matched the rhetoric in support of a legal shared parenting presumption, a number of countries and states have enacted equal or shared parenting legislation or are actively considering the reform of their family law statutes, in the direction of an equal or shared parenting presumption. Europe, Australia, and the United States are the vanguard in this regard; in Europe in particular, several countries have enacted some form of equal or shared parenting law, including the Netherlands, Belgium, and Denmark, and others are in the process of enacting such legislation. The jurisdictions chosen for review here reveal a diversity of approaches to the legal determination of parenting after divorce around the globe, and include the United States, United Kingdom, France, Sweden, and Australia.

United States

In the United States, parenting after divorce is under state, not federal, jurisdiction, and a number of states have now enacted some form of a presumption in favour of joint custody or shared parenting: Arizona, Iowa, Wisconsin, California, Connecticut, the District of Columbia, Florida, Idaho, Louisiana, Minnesota, Mississippi, New Hampshire, New Mexico, Oregon, and Wisconsin (American Bar Association 2010). Wisconsin's statute is one of the strongest: "the court shall presume that joint legal custody is in the best interest of the child" (Wisconsin Statutes 2011–12, Section 767). In Arizona, legislation requires that courts "maximize parenting time between the two parents and order shared legal decision-making" (Title 25: Marital and Domestic Relations, Chapter 4), and establishes maximum parenting time for both parents as a criterion in the determination of children's best interests, alongside the mental and physical capacity of parents, presence of domestic violence, and children's adjustment to divorce. Iowa has moved toward a joint custody presumption, with a statute that reads: "If joint legal custody is awarded to both parents, the court may award joint physical care to both joint custodial parents upon the request of either parent. If the court denies the request for joint physical care, the determination shall be accompanied by specific findings of fact and conclusions of law that the awarding of joint physical care is not in the best interest of the child." Kansas has legislated that "joint physical custody is the first order of preference" (Kansas Family Law Code 2012, Article 32). Oklahoma requires that, "the court shall provide substantially equal access to both parents ... unless the court finds that such shared parenting would be detrimental to the child. The burden of proof that such shared parenting would be detrimental to the child shall be upon the parent requesting sole custody" (Oklahoma Statutes, Title 43). In Texas, the Family Code contains a presumption of "joint conservatorship," which provides a minimum of 42% time with the non-custodial parent; by exercising other parts of Texas statutes, the time allocation may be extended to 50% (Texas Family Code, Chapter 153). Arkansas stipulates that "when in the best interests of the child, custody shall be awarded ... to ensure the frequent and continuing contact of the child with both parents" (Arkansas Code 2010, Title 9: Family Law, Subtitle 2, Chapter 13).

Overall, however, the United States is a study in contrasts in the area of custody and access legislation: twenty states include "frequent and continuing contact with both parents" or similar language; two utilize case law; three have only a preference for joint legal custody; seven presume joint custody when both parents agree; and thirteen have no statutes that promote shared parenting. Only one state, West Virginia, has adopted the "approximation standard," a form of equal parenting legislation which presumes that in contested cases the relative proportion of time children spend with each parent after divorce will be equal to the relative proportion of time each parent spent performing child caregiving functions before divorce.

The State of Washington is unique and a model state in parenting after divorce legislation, as the primary legal tool used to structure post-divorce parenting is the "parenting plan." When divorcing parents are unable to agree on parenting arrangements and court proceedings are necessary, a court order is made in the form of a "parenting plan." Parents are expected to have negotiated a plan prior to any court hearing on matters concerning their children. The parenting plan is the vehicle by which "parenting functions" are allocated between parents. These parenting functions include maintaining a stable, consistent, and nurturing relationship with the child, attending to the daily needs of the child, attending to the child's education, and providing financial support for the child. While there appears to be strong social political support for the Washington State Parenting Act, passed in 1987, the act does not appear to have had a significant impact on the reality of post-divorce parenting. For the most part, children continue to live with one parent following divorce and it is that parent who exercises control over significant decisions concerning the child; litigation rates have not substantially declined. Thus, it appears that parenting plans by themselves, without an equal or shared parenting presumption, may have little effect on post-divorce family structures or parental conflict levels.

United Kingdom

The United Kingdom's Children's Act (1989), which came into effect in 1991, replaced the terms "custody" and "access" with the terms "parental responsibility," "residence," and "contact." The central feature of the United Kingdom model of legal determination of parenting after divorce is the notion of "parental responsibility." The Act replaces the previous custody and access orders with four types of orders: residence orders, contact orders, specific issues orders, and prohibited steps orders. Essentially, the Children's Act changes the legal language of divorce.

The Children's Act declares that "the welfare of the child is paramount" in family law, and the child's welfare is "best served by maintaining as good a relationship with both parents as possible." Toward this end, "shared residence should be the common form of order" (Section 11 (4)). Yet there is no presumption of shared parenting or joint physical custody made in the Act, and court-determined outcomes, despite the Act's encouragement of the child's maintaining a relationship with both parents, reflect in practice a maternal preference presumption. Although the Act has provided for the option of shared parenting, this is not being applied consistently, and judicial discretion still leans toward the "tender years" doctrine and sole maternal custody as being in children's best interests.

As a critical tool in reducing conflict between parents and thereby ensuring better outcomes for children, the Children's Act stresses the importance of services geared toward parent education in the divorce process; this is referred to by some as "divorce gospel style" (Freeman 1997). Research indicates that the Act has not succeeded in reducing litigation concerning custody and access. Clearly, parent education and language changes in themselves will have limited positive effects.

As in Canada, a private member's bill was introduced in the United Kingdom to amend the Children's Act to provide for the making of shared parenting orders and to create a presumption that such orders enhance the welfare of the child. The present Conservative-Liberal Democrat coalition government has made a public commitment to a full review of family law with a view to facilitating greater involvement of both parents in children's lives, including a shared parenting consultation.

In November 2012, the UK government responded to the shared parenting consultation, in which respondents were asked

to consider the potential of four different approaches to promote post-separation shared parenting, with views on the impact
of this legislation. Most respondents favoured the shared-
parenting-presumption approach. The Family Justice Review
Panel, however, recommended against introducing legislation to
promote shared parenting, on the grounds that it risked creating
a perception of a parental right to shared or equal care. (It may
be noted, however, that recent Australian family legislation,
which created such a "parental rights" perception, led to positive outcomes overall.) The government planned to introduce
"parenting agreements which will set out the arrangements for
the child's care following family separation" (UK Department
for Education 2012, 5), and report on family law enforcement.
The government finally decided to presume that a child's welfare
will be furthered by the involvement of each of the child's parents in his or her life, unless it can be shown that such involvement would not in fact further the child's welfare: "even where
a parent can be involved without posing a risk of harm to the
child, the presumption will be rebutted if the court believes that
the parent's involvement is not consistent with the child's welfare" (UK Parliament 2012).

France

With respect to children, the principle of gender equality is
enshrined in virtually all statutes in France, a country with a civil
law tradition. In recent years, France has undertaken a significant
reform of its family law. While seeking to consider more effectively the diversity of family situations, the notions of "parental
responsibility" and "parental authority" are central in its recent
family law reforms which seek to "humanize and pacify divorce
proceedings, in order to provide parents with better support and
to create conditions for an organization responsible for the consequences of the parents' separation for the children" (Federal-
Provincial-Territorial Family Law Committee 2002, 79).

Law No. 2002-305 concerning parental authority, introduced
in 2002, was adopted by the French National Assembly in 2005.
This new shared parenting legislation seeks to promote the active

participation of both parents in the lives of their children after divorce. The law states: "Parents have more than just responsibilities; they also have a 'duty of requirement' in regard to their children, to enable the children to become socialized. Devaluing this duty would be to weaken the meaning of the parental relationship" (ibid, 80). In other words, parents' rights are regarded as legally necessary to enable them to successfully carry out their parental responsibilities. The French Civil Code encourages parents to agree on an "alternating residence" solution and grants the power for the court to impose such a solution. French law does not contain any legal presumption, yet the new law formally recognizes shared parenting as "alternating residence for the child after separation or divorce," and favours this mode of post-divorce family organization; parental authority is exercised jointly and the child resides with both parents on an alternating basis. In the words of the Dekeuwer-Défossez Commission, which concludes that the new legislation avoids one parent's rights being opposed to the other's: "Taking the child rather than the parents as the starting point, the text establishes the child's right to be raised by both parents and to preserve personal relations with each of them" (Federal-Provincial-Territorial Family Law Committee 2002, 83). The law also applies the principle of joint parenthood in cases of parental relocation of residence. In sum, parental authority and the responsibility of state institutions to respect that authority are key ingredients of this unique and reportedly successful shared-parental-responsibility approach to parenting after divorce.

France was also the site of the Langeac Declaration of Family Rights and Equal Parenting, signed in July 1999 by representatives of parents' groups from around the world. The declaration emphasizes that equal parenting laws should not be lengthy, intricate, or inaccessible to parents and children.

Belgium and the Netherlands

Belgium is considered to have a strong form of equal parenting legislation, with family law providing for equally divided, alternating residence of children whose parents are divorced, with enforcement measures in place to regulate equal parenting orders.

In Belgium, equal parenting is now established as the norm for divorced parents in conflict over parenting after divorce. In the Netherlands, the law has established a norm of joint legal parental authority over children after divorce, resulting in a significant increase in equal and shared parenting orders and arrangements, from a 5% rate of shared residential arrangements when the law first took effect in 1998, to 16% in 2008. In 2009 the Dutch parliament was scheduled to introduce new legislation that stipulated that a child is entitled to equal care by both parents after divorce, following the Belgian 50–50 norm, but after lengthy discussions the initiative was abandoned, and a parenting plan approach to the establishment of shared parental responsibility in disputed cases was put in its place.

Sweden and Denmark

A distinctive feature of Sweden's Children and Parents Code is its emphasis on parents having joint responsibility for their children, and one of the aims of recent amendments to the legislation has been to pave the way for more frequent application of joint custody arrangements. The court has the power to order joint custody against the wishes of the parents; the court can decide on joint custody or refuse to dissolve joint custody even though one of the parents may be opposed. Joint custody against the will of one of the parents is precluded if the other parent is subjecting a member of the family to violence, harassment, or other abusive treatment. Above all else, the court must take particular account of the child's need for "close and good contact with both parents." This legislation has resulted in a significant increase in equal and shared parenting arrangements after divorce in both contested and non-contested parenting after divorce cases.

Similarly, in Denmark, equal parenting legislation enacted in 2007 has resulted in a marked increase in equal and shared parenting arrangements. The Parental Responsibility Act established a default 50–50 equal parenting presumption for children of divorced parents who are unable to agree on parenting arrangements. Approximately 20% of children of divorce in both Denmark and Sweden are now living in equal or shared arrangements.

Australia

In Australia, discussions about joint custody and shared parental responsibility have been at the forefront of proposed family law changes for the past two decades. Despite the creation of a new Family Law Act in 1995, modelled largely on the United Kingdom's Children's Act (1989), its merely cosmetic changes to the language of divorce legislation, such as "primary residence" and "parental responsibility" taking the place of "custody," and "contact" replacing "access," were insufficient to meet its objective of decreasing litigation and conflict in family matters.

Despite reports that cite the 1995 Australian legislation as a failed example of a shared parenting or joint-physical-custody presumption, Australia has only recently opted to move toward a true shared-parental-responsibility approach. The report of the House of Representatives Standing Committee on Family and Community Affairs, *Every Picture Tells a Story*, was tabled in 2003, and contained the following recommendations regarding the amendment of the Family Law Act to: (1) create a clear, rebuttable presumption of equal shared parental responsibility, except where there is "entrenched" conflict, family violence, substance abuse, or established child abuse; (2) require mediators, counsellors, and legal advisors to assist parents to develop a parenting plan; (3) require courts and tribunals to consider substantially shared parenting time first when making orders in cases in which each parent wishes to be the primary caregiver; (4) replace the language of "residence" and "contact" with "parenting time"; and (5) create a network of Family Relationship Centres across the country to provide alternative dispute resolution services. In response to the report's recommendations, the Family Law Amendment (Shared Parental Responsibility) Bill 2005 was introduced.

The Family Law Amendment (Shared Parental Responsibility) Bill 2005 was enacted in March 2006. The law provides a presumption of equal shared parental responsibility, and requires courts to consider equal time in the first instance in parenting disputes after separation and divorce. The bill was designed, along with a proposed national network of Family Relationships Centres, to avoid litigation as the means of arriving at arrangements for the parenting of children after divorce. Its principal revision to the former Family Law Act is not only the establishment of equal shared parental responsibility as a presumption, but also a stated recognition that this is in the best interests of children after parental divorce. The main provisions of the new act are: (1) in implementing shared parental responsibility, the court will first consider "equal parenting time" and, if that is not feasible, then "substantial and significant parenting time with both parents" (considerations in this regard include geographical proximity of the parents, parenting capacity for equal time, parental communication capacity, and impact on the child); (2) the best interests of the child are comprised of "primary" and "additional considerations." Primary considerations include the child having a meaningful relationship with both parents, and the need to protect the child from physical and psychological harm, abuse, or family violence; additional considerations take into account the child's expressed views, and the relationship of the child with other persons, including grandparents and other relatives; (3) the obligation to attend family dispute resolution counselling before a parenting order is applied for; and (4) exempt are cases in which there are reasonable grounds to believe that there has been abuse of the child or family violence.

Although the Australian legislation stipulates that when making a parenting order, the court "must apply a presumption that it is in the best interests of the child for the child's parents to have equal shared parenting responsibility for the child" (Parliament of Australia 2006), equal parenting may be judged to not be in the best interests of the child. This applies not only when there are reasonable grounds to believe that child abuse or family violence has occurred, but covers a range of additional considerations, including children's views, changes to the family's circumstances, parental capacity, and other factors. As a result of this best-interests clause, judges have not significantly changed their practice of awarding sole residency, and there has been at best a modest increase in shared or equal parenting awards, when custody is contested. Court orders for shared care (defined as a minimum of 35% time with each parent) in litigated cases stand at only 12.6% today. Orders for shared care in both judicially determined and consent cases have increased from 9.1% prior to the reforms to 14.2% afterwards; the rate of equal parenting orders (as required by law) stands at only 7%. In one-third of litigated cases, the Australian court ordered that children spend less than 30% time with one of their parents; only 29% of these cases involved allegations of abuse or violence, and far fewer involved any finding of abuse. Thus, although the Australian legislation has moved toward the institutionalization of equal parenting, and although the legislation has had positive effects on non-litigated cases, it still has a ways to go.

The new Australian legislation has been closely monitored by the government, which released its report of the effectiveness of the new law in 2009 (Kaspiew et al 2009). The judicial and legal communities, long opposed to equal parenting legislation, have also commissioned research groomed to reflect the interests and concerns of these constituencies. There are some notable differences between the formal evaluation of the Australian reforms, commissioned by government and conducted by the Australian Institute for Family Studies (AIFS) (Kaspiew et al 2009), and the plethora of studies completed by those opposed to the reforms. The results of the latter (McIntosh and Chisolm 2009; Chisolm 2009; Hart and Bagshaw 2008) relying on small, unrepresentative samples, or data sets in which only custodial parents' views were sought, coincide neither with the more comprehensive and representative AIFS study, nor with most current North American research on parenting after divorce.

The results of the AIFS research indicate that equal parenting has widespread support from both parents and divorce practitioners, and works well when it is applied to the bulk of divorcing families in which violence has been not a factor in the marital relationship. Eighty-one percent of parents whose children were ordered into equal shared care arrangements, including those with very young children, reported that the arrangement was beneficial and working well for their children. Families with sole custody arrangements in which non-resident parents had disengaged from their children's lives reported the highest levels of child dysfunction. Most parents believe that spending half the time with each parent is appropriate, even for children under the age of three. A marked reduction in child custody litigation has also been noted since the new legislation, with applications to court over child custody falling by a staggering 72%. Court-determined parenting arrangements fell from 7.8% to 2.8% of cases, and lawyer negotiation from 10.6% to 5.8% of cases. Corresponding to decreased litigation has been a marked increase in the use of family relationship centres and family mediation services. And most Australian parents (72%) now resolve parenting arrangements without the use of any legal services.

Although the AIFS study found that shared care arrangements are sometimes ordered when parents have safety concerns regarding their children, it also found no evidence that high parental conflict had a more negative effect for children in shared care than for children in sole custody arrangements. Equal parenting arrangements, defined as children spending equal time in each parent's household, were also highly durable, more so than shared parenting arrangements (defined in Australian law as children spending at least 35% of time in each parent's household).

Chisolm (2009), McIntosh and Chisolm (2009), and Hart and Bagshaw (2008) caution against the application of equal shared parenting responsibility in cases of high conflict between parents, concluding that shared parenting is misused by courts to appease warring parties, prevailing over children's need for safety. They also recommend a presumption of no contact between an alleged perpetrator and child in all cases where domestic violence is alleged, and that allegations and denials of family violence should be listened to and taken seriously by family law professionals, and investigated by professionals with appropriate expertise, in a timely manner.

New developments in divorce law reform and the legal determination of parenting after divorce have been much slower in Canada than abroad. Across the globe, the option of equal and shared parenting has emerged as the logical next step in the ongoing evolution of parenting values and norms, and of family and socio-legal policy after parental divorce. Although full legal endorsement of equal parenting as a presumption is still relatively rare, and the notion that courts must retain their discretionary authority in determining the best interests of the child in contested cases remains, there is little doubt that a major paradigm shift has occurred in the law concerning parenting after divorce during the past twenty years in the western world. The "indissolubility of parenthood" (Parkinson and Cashmore 2011) reflects a growing awareness that although marital relationships may be freely dissoluble, parenthood is not. And as jurisdictions around the globe reform family law in the direction of an equal or shared parenting presumption, shared residential arrangements are emerging as a norm among divorced families worldwide.

4

The Discretionary Best-Interests Standard and the Primary Residence Model

As reflected in government reports prepared by socio-legal scholars, and a recent policy statement by the Canadian Bar Association, the Canadian legal community largely opposes an equal or shared parenting presumption (Cohen and Gershbain 2001; Canadian Bar Association 2010), and strongly endorses retaining the discretionary best-interests-of-the-child standard as the primary criterion in the legal determination of parenting after divorce, and child custody and access, in contested cases. This chapter will critically examine the notion that children's best interests and well-being after divorce are best served by sole custody or primary residence judgments, and provides a detailed overview of arguments for and against the discretionary best-interests-of-the-child standard in the legal determination of parenting after divorce.

CURRENT RESEARCH ON THE PRIMARY RESIDENCE MODEL

Until recently, the winner-take-all sole custody model had, surprisingly, come under relatively little scrutiny in either research or government reports. Joan Kelly (1991, 55) writes:

> It is ironic, and of some interest, that we have subjected joint custody to a level and intensity of scrutiny that was never directed toward the traditional post-divorce arrangement

(sole legal and physical custody to the mother and two weekends each month of visiting to the father). Developmental and relationship theory should have alerted the mental health field to the potential immediate and long-range consequences for the child of only seeing a parent four days each month. And yet until recently, there was no particular challenge to this traditional post-divorce parenting arrangement, despite growing evidence that such post-divorce relationships were not sufficiently nurturing or stabilizing for many children and parents. There is evidence that in our well-meaning efforts to save children in the immediate post-divorce period from anxiety, confusion, and the normative divorce-engendered conflict, we have set the stage in the longer run for the more ominous symptoms of anger, depression, and a deep sense of loss by depriving the child of the opportunity to maintain a full relationship with each parent.

Herein lies the crux of current child custody and access policy debates. It has somehow come to be regarded as developmentally "correct" to award primary residence to one parent, usually the mother, with twice-monthly weekend "contact" with the other parent, usually the father. There is mounting evidence, however, that such an arrangement disregards children's physical, psychological, and social needs for the active and meaningful involvement of both parents in their lives.

The focus of current child custody debates is on cases in which courts impose a de facto sole custody or primary residence criterion. The rights-based claims of mothers' and fathers' rights groups in this realm have led to an impasse and a state of confusion as to what exactly constitutes the best interests of children in divorce (Mason 1994). Judges have consistently awarded primary residence in contested cases, but their reasons for judgment – their interpretations of the best-interests-of-the-child standard – vary tremendously (ibid). The high potential of judicial bias in sole-custody-oriented parenting after divorce disputes results from the fact that judges are not trained in the complexities of child development and family dynamics (Woodhouse 1999).

In Canada, as in other jurisdictions, judges have maintained a "deficit" perspective of divorcing parents, asserting that shared parenting is unworkable in situations in which parents are in conflict and are therefore incapable of co-operation (Department of Justice Canada 1990; Mason 1994), and routinely impose primary residence orders. To the degree that a winner-take-all sole custody/primary residence approach is established, the adversarial system polarizes and disconnects the parties in dispute, exacerbating their conflict, and the problem of judicial bias as reflected in the imposition of sole custody and primary residence orders remains unaddressed.

To restructure the way parenting after divorce is legally determined, away from antiquated notions of sole custody and its offspring – primary residence and adversarial resolution – alternatives to sole custody are urgently needed. Three recent approaches have been tried both domestically and internationally: parent education programs for divorcing parents; changing the legal language in divorce law to make it less adversarial; and expanding professional programs and services, such as the number of family law judges, and promoting options such as family mediation, collaborative law, and parenting coordination.

The purpose of "divorce gospel-style" (Freeman 1997) – encouraging or mandating parents to use divorce education programs – is to emphasize the importance of children's well-being during the divorce transition, educate parents about children's best interests in divorce, and explain the divorce process, including alternative dispute resolution options. The weakness of such programs, however, is that they have relatively little impact on couples in conflict over the post-divorce parenting of their children; US- and UK-based research and experience bears this out (Braver et al 1996). Changing the legal language to make it appear less adversarial has similarly had little effect in jurisdictions such as the United Kingdom, Australia, and several US states; changing language alone does not change people's behaviour. And more programs and professional services are also in themselves not the answer; despite the burgeoning "divorce industry," the provision of more programs has not reduced inter-parental conflict in divorce (ibid). These reforms have neither significantly lessened the adversarial climate surrounding child custody, nor addressed the problem of judicial discretion in an area where judges lack the necessary knowledge of child development and family systems theory to begin to address complex child and family matters.

The proponents of an alternative approach to the legal determination of parenting after divorce argue that more radical reforms are needed which go well beyond the "cosmetic" family law reforms enacted thus far. Fundamental changes in divorce law, policy, and practice are required, including clear rules and guidelines to limit judicial discretion in an area in which judges have no formal training, and to lessen the adversarial climate that exacerbates parental conflict in divorce.

Four options have been advanced as alternative approaches to the present-day discretionary best-interests-of-the-child standard in the legal determination of parenting after divorce. First is the primary caregiver presumption, which would give a priori preference to the parent who is designated as primary in the child's life, usually defined as the parent who is providing more of the daily care of the children. In most instances, this position is based on the traditional role of the mother as the sole or primary caretaker of children. Thus, although touted as a gender-neutral standard, the primary caregiver presumption is essentially a sole-maternal-custody presumption as it assumes the presence of only one primary parent, which does not reflect the reality of most Canadian families with children (Higgins and Duxbury 2012). Child development research has demonstrated that children form strong and "primary" attachment bonds with both parents, even when caregiving is not equally shared (Rutter 1995); both mothers and fathers are salient individuals in their children's lives, and have a unique role to play in their development (Lamb 2010). Upon divorce, this is reflected in children's persistent yearning for their absent fathers; a critical factor in children's positive post-divorce adjustment is the maintenance of ongoing and meaningful relationships with both parents. The biggest problem with the primary caretaker presumption, however, relates to the question of how the court is to determine who is the "primary" parent: what is the basis for distinguishing "primary" versus "secondary" parenting? Equating the amount of time a parent spends with the child with that parent's importance in the child's life may be problematic, according to Warshak (2003b, 125): "Is the primary parent the parent who does the most to foster the child's sense of security, the person the child turns to in times of stress, the role that we most often associate with mothers? Or is it the parent who does the most to promote the child's ability to meet demands in the world outside the family, to make independent judgments, the role that we most often associate with fathers?" The emergent view among child development theorists is that in the majority of families, there is no basis for preferring one contribution to the other; both parents have a unique and primary contribution to make. It should be acknowledged, however, that the amount of time each parent spent with his or her children before divorce is a salient consideration for children's well-being, and thus it is advisable that a post-divorce parent-child living arrangement that is roughly equal in proportionate parental time to pre-divorce patterns be established post-divorce.

A second law reform option in the arena of parenting after divorce is thus the "approximation standard," whereby the caregiving status quo prior to divorce would prevail in contested cases. This approach sets out a legal expectation that post-divorce parenting arrangements reflect pre-divorce parenting patterns, an arrangement endorsed by the American Legal Institute. Critics have pointed to the difficulties of legally establishing the degree of child care involvement by parents prior to divorce, as judges tend to focus on child care arrangements in the immediate past, which may result from one parent withholding the child from the other parent to establish a caregiving status quo in contested custody cases. Critics also note that litigation rates would likely not decrease with such a formula. However, to the degree that the approximation standard seeks to maintain stability in children's relationships with their parents, it does have merit, and could serve as a useful guideline for parents seeking to minimize disruption and maintain consistency in children's routines following separation and divorce.

Third, a legal joint custody presumption has been advanced, within which parents share decision-making responsibility for, but not necessarily physical care of, their children after divorce. Feminist scholars (Polikoff 1982), however, have pointed to the inequity and power imbalance that may result in giving one parent decision-making authority over their child (and former spouse) without any corresponding obligation for child care on the part of that parent. In practice, this approach is routinely applied as Canadian courts grant sole physical custody with joint decision-making authority in contested cases. Some non-residential parents have characterized this approach as "joint custody in name only," as their primary interest is their children's need for both parents being involved as caregivers in their lives (Kruk 2010a).

The fourth option, equal or shared parental responsibility (also referred to as a rebuttable presumption of physical joint custody), would grant both parents equal or shared decision-making authority and equal or shared child care responsibility. This option appears to be the most viable alternative to the sole custody model inasmuch as it overcomes the main limitations of the three approaches above, and will thus be the focus of the chapters following.

Family law systems which uphold a sole custody, primary residence, or primary parent criterion have not been subject to the same level of scrutiny as alternative approaches such as equal or shared parental responsibility. Yet in research studies on the views of children and parents negatively affected by divorce (Kruk 2010a; Kruk 2010b; Fabricius 2003), the message is clear: the sole custody system is the problem. And although in situations in which parents embroiled in a custody contest are characterized as unable or unwilling to remain focused on their children's needs and interests, with a "parent-blaming" tone and "parent-deficit" perspective applied to uphold the discretionary best-interests-of-the-child standard, a strengths-based approach building on parental strengths provides another perspective to post-divorce parenting. The starting points of a strengths-based approach are the perspectives of children and parents themselves on the matter of children's best interests during and after divorce.

THE DISCRETIONARY
BEST-INTERESTS-OF-THE-CHILD STANDARD

Currently in most western states, the best interests of the child remains as the sole or primary criterion upon which legal determinations of parenting after divorce are based. Indeed, it is asserted that assessing each case on its own merits, especially considering the individualized justice and flexibility afforded by the best-interests-of-the-child standard, should be the cornerstone of modern family law. This standard provides the background or context within which any attempts at law reform must be situated.

Yet, the perspectives of children and parents themselves are largely absent in current analyses of the best-interests-of-the-child concept. Increasingly, this has become primarily the bailiwick of legal scholars. The legal best-interests-of-the-child criterion is touted as egalitarian and gender-neutral, flexible, and simple to apply. The Canadian Bar Association, in declaring its position strongly in favour of the standard, asserts that whereas one-shoe-fits-all legal child custody presumptions typically focus on parental rights, the best-interests-of-the-child standard is clearly focused on children's interests. It is claimed that the standard provides a safety net of considerations for the court to ensure that children's safety and well-being are protected to the maximum degree possible. In addition, in allowing judges to exercise their discretion based on the individual parents and children in the case before them, the best-interests-of-the-child standard provides for individual justice for each individual child whose parents are in dispute; each case may be evaluated on its individual set of facts with a full evaluation of each child's and parent's unique circumstances. Further, it is argued that social science research has not established the amount of parent-child contact necessary to maintain child well-being, and since conflicted parents are considered to pose a risk to children's psychological health after divorce, courts must retain their discretionary function in adjudicating children's best interests in individual cases. Finally, courts should be able to apply discretion in cases in which there are allegations of abuse but in which there may be insufficient admissible evidence to support the allegations.

These claims, however, are not supported by empirical research. For example, current data indicate that judges do not fine-tune their decisions to parenting patterns that existed before divorce, but rather base their decisions on gender, continuing to use a gender-based stereotype of mothers as providing superior "tender years" care (Millar 2010; Kruk 2008). Fathers and mothers not conforming to this stereotype are particularly at risk of losing primary residence in the courts (ibid). The "gender paradigm" (Dutton and Nicholls 2005) dominates child custody decision-making in Canada, reinforced by flawed and misleading judicial education on child custody and domestic violence (Brown 2004; Dutton and Nicholls 2005).

A number of commentators have advanced proposals for strengthening the best-interests-of-the-child criterion, to include a list of criteria or a definition of the best interests of the child, to guide judges and parents applying the test. Without being exhaustive, such a list would set out all of the criteria that decision-makers should consider. The presence of a list of guiding criteria, it is argued, would improve the predictability of results, and encourage consideration of factors considered particularly important to the well-being of the child. Guiding criteria may include the caregiving role assumed by each parent during the child's life, any past history of family violence perpetrated by any party applying for custody or access, the child's established cultural ties and religious affiliation, and the importance and benefit to children of having an ongoing relationship with both of their parents.

Despite efforts to standardize best-interests-of-the-child criteria, it is now acknowledged that in contested child custody, the ideals of individualized justice and individual decision-making, on the one hand, and uniform standards and predictability in decision-making, on the other, are extremely difficult to combine, and the development of guiding criteria vis-à-vis the best interests of the child in the legal determination of parenting after divorce remain elusive.

Nine Arguments against the Discretionary Best-Interests Standard

It is the indeterminacy of the best-interests-of-the-child standard that is its main downfall, as the absence of a clear definition or consensus on children's best interests renders the standard unworkable. Nine arguments against the principle that the discretionary best interests of the child ought to be the sole, main, or first and paramount framework for child custody determination may be advanced, as follows:

1 The best-interests-of-the-child standard is vague and indeterminate.
2 The best-interests-of-the-child standard is subject to judicial error.
3 Best-interests-of-the-child-based decisions reflect a sole custody presumption and judicial bias.
4 The best-interests-of-the-child standard sustains, intensifies, and creates conflict, and fuels litigation.
5 The best-interests-of-the-child standard makes the court dependent on custody evaluations lacking an empirical foundation.
6 The views of children and parents regarding the best interests of the child are radically different to those of the judiciary.
7 The best-interests-of-the-child standard is a smokescreen for the underlying issue of the judiciary and the legal system retaining their decision-making power in the child custody realm.
8 Contrary to the UN Convention on the Rights of the Child, Canadian children of divorce are discriminated against on the basis of parental status in regard to the removal of their parents from their lives.
9 Despite the rhetoric of the best interests of the child, the parties in best-interests proceedings are usually parents whose legal counsel represents the interests of parents, not the children. When parental and child interests clash, parents' lawyers are bound to represent the interests of their clients, over and above the interests of (usually unrepresented) children.

1 *The best-interests-of-the-child standard is vague and indeterminate.* The vagueness and indeterminacy of the best-interests-of-the-child standard gives unfettered discretion to judges not trained in child development and family dynamics, resulting in unpredictable and inconsistent outcomes based on idiosyncratic biases and subjective, value-based judgments.

The best-interests-of-the-child standard has a certain cadence and seems caring and humane, a noble aspiration, writes O'Connell (2007), but is a trap for the unwary. Increasingly, the best-interests-of-the-child standard has come under scrutiny by legal scholars concerned about the unpredictability of judicial rulings as a result of its vagueness (Woodhouse 1999). Given the lack of training of judges in child development and family dynamics, the Family Law Education Review Commission, which oversees law school curricula in the United States, concluded that judges are not equipped to make decisions about the best interests of children in regard to custody or parenting plans. Children's best interests have been left undefined, lacking legal consensus, based on speculation about future conduct, and lacking clear guidelines for their assessment (Emery, Otto, and O'Donohue 2005). Thus, judges' views on the best interests of the child are highly variable, and outcomes are unpredictable and inconsistent; the inherent ambiguity of the best-interests standard can only lead to judicial subjectivity regarding its application, resulting in adjudication based on personal bias and beliefs rather than clear statutory guidelines (Shuman and Berk 2012). The best-interests-of-the-child standard is essentially a projective test, and the absence of a clear definition of or judicial consensus on children's best interests renders it unworkable (Emery 2007). Courts thus cannot determine a child's best interests with certainty, and judges are forced to rely on their own interpretations of children's interests. Idiosyncratic biases and subjective value-based judgments, including gender bias, replace objective considerations. Judges must choose between specific views and values regarding child-rearing, usually favouring litigants with values and attributes similar to their own (Warshak 2007). They also fall prey to the influence of various rights-based lobbies, such as those representing one or the other gender in the "custody wars" (Mason 1996). However, when two "good enough" parents are in dispute over post-divorce parenting arrangements, there is no basis in either law or psychology for choosing one parent over the other as a custodial or residential parent (Kelly and Johnston 2005). In most instances, there is simply no rational basis for preferring one parent to another.

According to Elster (1987), a determinative standard is needed, which requires the following conditions to be satisfied in respect to parenting after divorce: (1) all the parenting options available to the child and family must be known; (2) all the possible outcomes of each option must be known; (3) the probabilities of each outcome must be known; and (4) the values attached to each outcome must be known. The best-interests-of-the-child standard has failed to pass muster in each of these respects, and has remained "a standard with no standards" (Emery, Otto, and O'Donohue 2005, 19) for too long. A law that provides no effective judicial guidance is worse than no law at all because it leads to the arbitrary exercise of judicial power, the rule of judges rather than the rule of law.

2 *The best-interests-of-the-child standard is subject to judicial error.* Asked to make life-changing decisions based on a discretionary and subjective assessment of a multitude of factors, judges struggle to make accurate diagnoses of what will be in the long-term best interests of children. Information that is presented in court, with each party obfuscating his or her own character flaws and smearing the character of the other party, is thrice contaminated: first by the client when advising his or her lawyer; second by the lawyer when preparing an affidavit; and third by the judge who reads or retains selectively what is presented in court (Brown 2004). Cases are largely decided by the way evidence is presented in court, and thus the determination of the best interests of the child is subject to judicial error (Firestone and Weinstein 2004). At least in cases in which it is not glaringly obvious to an unbiased observer that one parent is more able and the other is less able, there is an appreciable risk that judges will

get it wrong; they will choose the less able parent as the primary caregiver. By hypothesis, this is the worst possible outcome, as these errors can have disastrous consequences, such as in cases in which sole custody is granted to an abusive or neglectful parent, or one who is determined to alienate the child from the non-custodial parent. Given the total authority which parents in sole custody situations are granted, the potential for child maltreatment, neglect, and abuse, in that context, is virtually unchecked. Justice for children is thus not served by the best-interests-of-the-child standard.

3 *Best-interests-of-the-child-based decisions reflect a sole custody presumption, with primary residence orders being the norm.* Although published reasons for judgments in contested child custody cases reveal a wide range of views and biases among judges regarding what they consider to be the best interests of children, judges are remarkably consistent in awarding sole custody or primary residence orders in contested cases. Most judges simply assume that in cases in which there is a trial over the issue, children's best interests are best served by awarding post-divorce care and control of children to one parent only. Decisions have, in the majority of cases, reflected the presumption that mothers are to care for children, while fathers provide financial support (Millar 2009; Millar and Goldenberg 1998). Although sole custody and primary residence judgments are associated with diminished parenting – a key factor in children's problematic adjustment to divorce – joint physical custody and equal or shared parenting are generally seen to be unworkable by the judiciary in cases in which parenting after divorce is in dispute, and such arrangements are therefore determined not to be in the best interests of children (ibid). The result is that when there is a trial, parents typically petition for primary residence, and with the high stakes involved in such a winner-take-all forum, family disputes are among the most bitter battles waged in court. An adversarial process prevails in which "winning" is the object of the exercise, as parents engage in character assassinations in an attempt to gain the upper hand in what becomes a contest over

the "custody" of children. Current practice thus promotes litigation, and as rules of evidence are applied in a highly flexible fashion, and as many and diverse factors may be considered relevant to a child's best interests, contested cases are increasingly complex, costly to litigate, and potentially harmful to all affected parties (Bala 2000).

4 *The best-interests-of-the-child standard sustains, intensifies and creates conflict, and fuels litigation.* The best-interests-of-the-child standard provides a fertile battleground for parents in disagreement over post-divorce parenting and catalyzes battles between parents. The uncertainty surrounding the best-interests-of-the-child standard sustains and intensifies conflict, fuels litigation, and in some cases leads to family violence. New research suggests that the hostility resulting from the divorce process is the strongest predictor of poor outcomes for children (Bonach 2005; Semple 2010); the adversarial and hostile nature of court proceedings has a very negative impact on post-divorce parenting relationships. Pruett and Jackson (1999) found that in 71% of cases, the legal process made custody litigants' feelings of anger and hostility more extreme, according to self-reports, and 75% indicated that the process intensified their negative perception of the other parent. Thus, the best-interests-of-the-child principle is self-defeating, as it increases the risk to children's and families' well-being by increasing the incidence of litigation and protracted and increased parental conflict. It also creates a dangerous incentive for strategic behaviour on the part of parents locked in a custody contest. That is, characterizing their dispute as "high conflict" becomes a weapon used by some parents in an attempt to deprive the other of legal custody or parenting time. Parents routinely portray their conflict as far more intractable than it actually is (Nielsen 2013).

5 *The best-interests-of-the-child standard makes the court dependent on custody evaluations lacking an empirical foundation.* The best-interests-of-the-child standard also makes the court largely dependent on the assessments of professional

custody evaluators. However, judicial reliance on expert testimony is highly problematic, as judges are not informed consumers of such evidence (Emery, Otto, and O'Donohue 2006; Shuman 2002; Shuman and Berk 2012), and the scientific basis for child custody evaluation is hotly contested (O'Connell 2007). Given the lack of an empirical foundation for such evaluation, child custody recommendations, it has been argued, are ethically problematic (Tippins and Wittman 2005).

6 *The views of children and parents regarding the best interests of the child are different to those of the judiciary.* On the issue of the best interests of the child, the views of children and parents, and the legal community and judiciary, stand in stark contrast (Pruett, Hoganbruen and Jackson 2000). Whereas judges focus on parental capacities and deficits when defining the best interests of the child, parents are oriented toward children's needs in the divorce transition. Contrary to the views of legal practitioners and the judiciary who focus on legal criteria respecting best interests, parents indicate that children's best interests are related to their psychological needs, stability and continuity in their routines and relationships, and the active and responsible involvement of both parents in their lives (ibid; Kruk 2010a; Kruk 2010b). Children are clear that their primary interest is maintaining meaningful relationships with both of their parents in equal measure (Fabricius 2003).

7 *The best-interests-of-the-child principle serves the interests of those in the judiciary and legal system who retain their decision-making power in the child custody realm.* Some have argued that the best-interests-of-the-child principle is in fact a smokescreen, as it is not in fact the best interests of children that is at issue, but who is to decide these interests. Legal practitioners and the judiciary do not wish to relinquish their power in the realm of child custody, as the livelihood of family law and allied professionals would be seriously threatened with a legal equal or shared parenting presumption, which would have the effect of enhancing determinacy and reducing litigation. The legal status

quo is thus vigorously defended. And case law and precedent prevail, despite societal changes in family roles and structures. Case law keeps looking back rather than advancing forward; the unnecessary legalization of human problems, disempowerment of parents, invasion of family privacy, delayed outcomes, and vast financial expense are all endemic to the discretionary best-interests-of-the-child model.

8 Children of divorce are discriminated against on the basis of parental status in regard to removal of their parents from their lives. An important point concerning the flaws of the best-interests-of-the-child standard that has been overlooked by most legal scholars relates to the fact that when sole custody or primary residence orders are made by the court, the court does not, as claimed, award custody to a parent after divorce; in actuality it removes legal custody from a parent, as custody is equally shared by parents before divorce. And in the act of removing custody via the discretionary best-interests-of-the-child standard, children of divorce are discriminated against on the basis of parental status. Whereas the removal of a parent from the life of a child in a two-parent family is subject to the child-in-need-of-protection test, a much more stringent standard than the best-interests principle in regard to parental removal, children of divorce are subject to an indeterminate standard vis-à-vis the protection of their relationships with each of their parents. Under the child-in-need-of-protection standard, a parent can only be removed as a custodial parent, and only as a last resort, when a finding is made that a child is in need of protection from a parent, subsequent to a comprehensive investigation, assessment, and recommendation by a competent child protection authority, rather than simply on the basis of judicial discretion when unproven allegations are made in family court, or parents are simply in disagreement over their children's living arrangements. Children of divorce are thus not afforded the same protection with respect to their relationships with each of their parents as are children in two-parent families. This is a double standard and contrary to the UN Convention on the Rights of the Child, Article 2, which stipulates that a child should be protected from all forms of discrimination, including the marital status of his or her parent. Additionally, Article 5 emphasizes the primacy of parents in their children's lives ("States Parties shall respect the responsibilities, rights and duties of parents"), Article 8 stipulates the child's right to preserve his or her family and cultural identity, and Article 9 states that children shall not be separated from their parents against their will. Article 18 indicates that both parents have the primary responsibility for the upbringing and development of the child, and States Parties shall render appropriate assistance to parents in the performance of their child-rearing responsibilities. Article 19 refers to needed measures to protect children from all forms of violence, injury or abuse, neglect, maltreatment, or exploitation – and it refers to actual violence and maltreatment, not risks of violence and maltreatment. To remove child custody from a parent because of perceived risk rather than proof of harm is not in keeping with the Convention.

9 *Despite the surrounding rhetoric of the best interests of the child, the parties in best-interests proceedings are usually parents whose legal counsel represents the interests of parents, not children. When parental and child interests clash, parents' lawyers are bound to represent the interests of their clients, over and above the interests of (usually unrepresented) children.*   A major flaw of the current system of child custody determination is the fact that children are left unrepresented in the proceedings, as the legal counsels of mothers and fathers are retained to further the interests of only two of the parties in the dispute (Semple 2010).

The needs and best interests of children of divorce have been subject to considerable research scrutiny, including children in both primary residential and equal and shared parenting arrangements. It has been clearly established that harm to children in the divorce aftermath results from broken attachments and parental estrangement, exposure to parental conflict, instability and discontinuity in children's routines, and a marked decline in children's standard of living. It is now generally accepted that the psychological distress of children of divorce is substantial, and related to the four factors above, particularly the first two (Kelly 2000; Lamb and Kelly 2001; Laumann-Billings and Emery 2000; Lamb, Sternberg, and Thompson 1997; Amato 2000; Booth 1999). Tragically, current outcomes in divorce are such that all four conditions are present for large numbers of children of divorce, particularly those who have been the subject of child custody litigation. A significant number of children have lost contact with their non-resident parents subsequent to divorce. Children are thus uprooted, as their primary attachments to one parent and set of kin are effectively severed; children's adjustment to divorce in "father-absent" situations in particular is highly problematic (Lamb, Sternberg, and Thompson 1997; Amato 2000; Booth 1999; Emery 1999). And whereas non-resident parents suffer the absence of their children, custodial parents, usually mothers, are overwhelmed by the assumption of sole responsibility for their children (Braver and O'Connell 1998). Conflict between parents does not abate in disputed cases, particularly those in which the court is involved in determining custody. Child poverty remains a pressing issue, as does women's traditional economic dependence on men, neither of which are effectively addressed within the sole custody / primary residence system.

Yet, sole custody continues in the form of primary residence awards, even in jurisdictions that have implemented shared parenting legislation which has fallen short of its original aims and thereby compromised its success. Shared parenting legislation in countries like Australia, for example, as discussed in chapter 3, contains a number of qualifiers, such as the application of the indeterminate best-interests-of-the-child test to rebut the presumption, in place of clear, unambiguous, and firm guidelines. The result has been that equal and shared parenting is not being ordered in the majority of contested cases; in Australia, court orders for shared care in litigated cases stand at only 12.6% today, and the rate of equal parenting orders stands at only 7%.

The discretionary best-interests-of-the-child standard, despite being subject to the many criticisms outlined in this chapter, thus remains firmly entrenched in both family law statutes and in common law around the globe. The opposition of the judiciary and family law associations to any proposals that would limit judicial discretion in child custody matters is swift and firm, as in the case of the Canadian Bar Association's taking the justice minister to task over his party's stated support for a shared parenting presumption. And child development scholars have remained largely silent in regard to the implications of their research on children and families of divorce on family law and policy. I examine this research in the following chapter.

5

The Needs and Well-Being
of Children of Divorce:
Preservation of Parent-Child Relationships

RESEARCH ON CHILD OUTCOMES IN DIVORCE

Children's relationships with their parents play a crucial role in shaping their social, emotional, personal, and cognitive development, and there is substantial literature documenting the adverse effects of disrupted parent-child relationships on children's development and adjustment (Lamb 1999; Lamb et al 1999). The evidence further shows that children who are deprived of meaningful relationships with one of their parents are at greater risk psychologically, even when they are able to maintain good relationships with the other parent. Children are more likely to attain their psychological potential when they are able to develop and maintain meaningful relationships with both parents, whether the two parents live together or not. A large body of research documents the adverse effects of severed father-child relationships in particular, including father-infant relationships (Lamb et al 1999).

Two benchmark longitudinal studies on children's needs in the separation and divorce transition followed cohorts of children of divorce from childhood to adulthood, and remain a key source of information about children's adjustment to the consequences of parental divorce. The main findings of Hetherington et al, beginning in 1978, a sophisticated study in the single-parent research tradition, and of Wallerstein and Kelly, starting in 1980, which utilized the perspectives and methods of clinical research with a sample of "normal" children and parents of divorce, tend to be corroborative. Both studies found that, particularly during the first year after divorce, the parenting capacities of both mothers and fathers deteriorate significantly. During divorce and after, parents tend to ascribe their own feelings to their children and are often unaware of and relatively insensitive to their children's needs. In the midst of their own feelings of anger, rejection, and bitterness, parents may not have the emotional capacity to cope with their children's feelings as well; the emotional strain engendered by the process of divorce is strongly associated with parental unresponsiveness to children's emotional needs. At the same time, children often deliberately hide their distress from their parents.

The multiple transitions that accompany divorce for parents affect children acutely. The form and severity of children's reactions depend on factors such as age, gender, and particular circumstances, and although some disagreement exists as to which age group tends to show which symptoms, studies continue to show that children of divorced families frequently exhibit behavioural difficulties, poor self-esteem, depression, and poor school performance.

Children of different ages and developmental stages react differently to separation and divorce; the stage of children's emotional development is an important factor in how they will perceive the divorce. Children under the age of five are the most adversely affected by the divorce transition. They manifest vulnerability to depression (the opposite is true for intact families), confusion about the nature of families and interpersonal relationships, a tendency to blame themselves for the divorce (which is highly resistant to therapeutic intervention), regression in behaviour and general development, a fear of being sent away or replaced, joyless play, a preoccupation with trying to fit objects together, and a yearning for the absent parent – and they are the group most at risk of losing contact with non-custodial fathers. Early-latency-age children exhibit a pervasive sadness and sense of loss, feelings of fear and insecurity, acute longing for the absent parent, and an intense desire for the reconciliation of their parents, believing that the intact family is absolutely necessary for their continued safety and growth. Late-latency-age children evidence feelings of shame and embarrassment, active attempts to reconcile their parents while trying to break up any new social relationships, divided loyalties and taking sides between the parents, conflicting feelings of grief and intense anger – usually directed toward the custodial parent (especially by boys) – and a two-level functioning (hiding their painful feelings in order to present a courageous front to the world). Adolescents show continuing anger, sadness, a sense of loss and betrayal, shame and embarrassment, and a concern about their own future marriages and relationships.

Wallerstein and Kelly found that no children under the age of thirteen in their sample wanted the divorce to happen. Mitchell (1985) obtained similar results: less than half of the children in her sample were even aware of any parental conflict within the marriage, and even those who had been aware of conflict thought their family life to have been happy and did not view their parents' conflict as a sufficient reason to divorce. Children who were unhappy prior to their parents' divorce were often so due to the implied threat of divorce. Wallerstein and Kelly also found that the degree of conflict within the marriage prior to the divorce was not related to children's post-divorce adjustment: marriages that were unhappy for the adults were generally perceived as comforting and gratifying for the children. Not only did children not concur with their parents' decision or express any relief at the time of divorce, but five years after, while adults were generally satisfied with having made the right decision, children still wished for the reconciliation of their parents and wanted to return to the pre-divorce state.

In recent years, studies have examined the specific factors associated with divorce that most trouble children. Both Wallerstein and Kelly, and Hetherington et al, concluded that the absence of the non-custodial parent is a very significant factor; they describe the intense longing of children for their non-custodial fathers: all of the 131 children in the Wallerstein and Kelly sample longed intensely for their father's return. Both studies found that two factors, the amount and severity of conflict between the parents, and the degree to which children are able to maintain meaningful relationships with each parent, play a major role in determining the outcome of divorce for children. They also found children being the focus of parental conflicts, children experiencing loyalty conflicts, one or both parents experiencing poor emotional health, parents lacking social supports, poor quality of parenting, lack of or inappropriate communication to children about the divorce, and child poverty are associated with the prolonged distress of children after divorce.

Since the groundbreaking research of Hetherington et al and Wallerstein and Kelly, Amato (2000) has provided an in-depth overview of five major perspectives that have been used in research to account for children's adjustment to divorce. These include the absence of the non-custodial parent, the adjustment of the custodial parent, inter-parental conflict, economic hardship, and stressful life changes. The most salient factor in children's adjustment, according to Amato, is the impact of inter-parental conflict. Amato proposed the development of a new "resources and stressors" model in understanding children's experience. This model suggests that children's development is facilitated by the possession of certain classes of resources (such as parental support and socio-economic resources). Parental divorce can be problematic because it involves a number of stressors that challenge children's development (such as inter-parental conflict and disruptive life changes) and because it can interfere with children's ability to utilize parental resources (through loss of contact with one parent and loss of access to income). According to Amato, the total configuration of resources and stressors, rather than the presence or absence of a particular factor, needs to be considered in any examination of the impact of divorce on children.

There has been considerable debate in the literature about whether children fare better in "stable," non-conflicted single-parent families with minimal or no contact with the non-custodial parent, or in situations in which they maintain regular contact with both parents but are exposed to ongoing inter-parental conflict. In cases in which high levels of conflict between parents persist after divorce, is it in children's best interests to maintain regular contact with both parents, or to limit or cease contact with one? A British study (Lund 1987) isolated the variables of parental harmony/conflict and father involvement/absence to assess their relative impact on children's post-divorce functioning. The study utilized a longitudinal design and multiple measures of children's adjustment. Interviewing both sets of parents (and also children's classroom teachers and others to gain an independent rating of children's post-divorce functioning), Lund divided post-divorce families into three groups: harmonious (or neutral) co-parents, conflicted co-parents, and single parent (or father-absent) families. Her results indicate that children fare best in harmonious co-parental families and fare least well in single parent father-absent families. The benefits of father involvement for children were evident in both the harmonious and conflicted co-parenting groups. Conflict between the parents was not as strong a predictor of poor outcome for children as was the absence of the father after divorce.

A large number of studies from the 1990s and early 2000s (Gunnoe and Braver 2002; Laumann-Billings and Emery 2000; Amato and Gilbreth 1999; Lamb 1999; Lamb, Sternberg, and Thompson 1997; Bender 1994; Warshak 1992; Maccoby and Mnookin 1992; Bisnaire, Firestone, and Rynard 1990) have demonstrated the salutary effects of dual parental involvement and shared parenting after divorce on children's divorce-specific and general adjustment. Kelly (2000), in reviewing a decade of research on child outcomes, concluded that joint custody led to better overall child outcomes, and that inter-parental conflict in itself was not detrimental to children, only child-focused conflict to which children were directly exposed proved to be detrimental. Kelly and Lamb (2000) found that, almost by definition, custody and access disputes involve "high conflict," but concluded that such (non-violent) conflict itself was not necessarily harmful. Amato (2000) concluded that divorce has significant negative impacts on children; however, moderating factors include children's coping skills and the presence of joint custody. Bauserman (2002) provided an in-depth meta-analysis of studies comparing child and parent outcomes in shared versus sole residential arrangements, concluding that children in shared parenting homes fare significantly better, on average, on all measures of heath and emotional well-being. None of these studies have found that children in sole custody fare better in their psychological and social adjustment than children in joint custody families; indeed, children in sole custody arrangements run a greater risk of academic problems, alcohol and drug use, poor social skills, depression and suicide, delinquency and incarceration, and poor physical health and early mortality.

There has been an explosion of interest and new empirical research over the past decade on the impact of shared parenting on child and family well-being (Bauserman 2012; Fabricius et al 2011 and 2010; Fabricius and Luecken 2007; Cashmore and Parkinson 2010; Bjarnason and Arnarsson 2012 and 2010; Spruijt and Duindan 2010; Kaspiew et al 2009; Melli and Brown 2008; Campana et al 2008; Jablonska and Lindberg 2007; Breivik and Olweus 2006; Neoh and Mellor 2010; Finley and Schwartz 2007), and a clearer picture has emerged that challenges a number of negative assumptions and misperceptions. There are now over two dozen studies on equal and shared parenting families that have uncovered important new data directly relevant to policymakers and legislators in the field of child custody. (These are discussed in detail in chapter 7.) Four important new findings are particularly relevant to the question of legal determination of parenting after divorce, as follows:

1 *Children of divorce want equal time with their parents, and consider equal or shared parenting to be in their best interests. Seventy percent of children of divorce believe that equal amounts of time with each parent is the best living arrangement for children, including 93% of children raised in equal-time homes; and children who had equal-time arrangements have the best relations with each of their parents after divorce.* Studies that have attempted to examine the issue of child custody from the

standpoint of children themselves have tended to rely on clinical samples (Wallerstein, Lewis, and Blakeslee 2000), or simply have neglected to ask children about their desires or needs respecting living arrangements (Smart 2002). A new large-scale (n=829) US study of children who have lived through their parents' divorces concludes that children want equal time with each of their parents, and consider shared parenting to be in their best interests, as well as in the best interests of children generally. Fabricius (2003) and Fabricius and Hall (2000) shed light on the child custody debate with their focus on the perspective of children in divorce. Three out of four young adults who grew up in divorced families thought that the best parenting plans were those that gave children equal time in each parent's home; the authors found that equal time is what most children desire and consider as being in their best interests. The authors sought the perspectives of young adults on their post-divorce living arrangements as children, and also gathered data from young adults who were children in non-divorced families. Their findings are consistent with earlier research focused directly on children of divorce (Lund 1987; Derevensky and Deschamps 1997); Parkinson, Cashmore, and Single (2003) also found that when children were asked about how parents should care for them after divorce, the most common answer specified equal-time arrangements. Fabricius (2003) and Fabricius and Hall (2000) compared children's actual post-divorce living arrangements with the living arrangement they wanted, the living arrangement their mothers wanted, the living arrangement their fathers wanted, the living arrangement they believed best for children of divorce, the living arrangement they believed best for children of divorce if both parents are good parents and live relatively close to each other, the relative number of days in a typical week with each parent they believe best for children of different ages experiencing their parents' divorce, how close they now felt toward their mothers and fathers, the degree of anger they now felt toward their mothers and fathers, the degree to which each of their parents wanted the other parent to be involved as a parent, and the degree to which each of their parents undermined the other parent as a parent. The authors noted that although children of divorce perceive a large gender gap in their parents' generation on the issue of child custody, there was no evidence of this gap in their own generation. As young adults who lived through the divorce of their parents, they are arguably, in a sense, the real "experts" on the best interests of children of divorce. They certainly felt an injustice in not being allowed to have an equal voice in the proceedings. Finally, Fabricius (2003) found that children in sole custody arrangements who experience a history of unavailability of the non-residential parent articulate feelings of insecurity in their relationship with that parent, have a perception of rejection by that parent, and feel anger toward both parents. Consistent with this finding, Amato and Gilbreth (1999), in their meta-analysis of the father-child post-divorce relationship, found that children who were less close to their fathers after divorce had poorer behavioural and emotional adjustment, and lower school achievement. Fabricius's discovery that equal parenting time is the stated preference of the majority of children of divorce has since been examined by other researchers, and this finding has emerged as one of the most consistent and robust in divorce research over the past decade (Finley and Schwartz 2007; Marquardt 2005; Parkinson, Cashmore, and Single 2005; Harvey and Fine 2010).

2 *Not only do children of divorce want equal time, but also equal time works. A meta-analytic review of the thirty-three major North American studies comparing sole with joint-physical-custody arrangements has shown that children in joint custody arrangements fare significantly better on all adjustment measures than children who live in sole custody arrangements.* This meta-analysis of the major North American studies over the past decade, which compares outcomes in joint versus sole custody homes, found that joint custody is associated with outcomes that are more salutary for children. Bauserman (2002) compared child adjustment in joint-physical-custody and joint-legal-custody settings with sole (maternal and paternal) custody settings, and also intact family settings. He examined children's general

adjustment, family relationships, self-esteem, emotional and behavioural adjustment, divorce-specific adjustment, as well as the degree and nature of ongoing conflict between parents. On every measure of adjustment, children in joint-physical-custody arrangements fared significantly better than children in sole custody arrangements: "Children in joint custody arrangements had less behaviour and emotional problems, had higher self-esteem, better family relations and school performance than children in sole custody arrangements" (Bauserman 2002, 91).

Although many of the studies reviewed by Bauserman compared self-selected joint custody families with sole custody families, some examined families with legally mandated joint-physical-custody arrangements, in which joint custody was ordered over the objections of at least one of the parents. These families fared as well as the self-selected samples, reinforcing the findings of earlier studies that joint custody works equally well for families in which parents are vying for custody and in conflict (Maccoby and Mnookin 1992; Benjamin and Irving 1989; Maccoby, Depner and Mnookin 1988; Brotsky, Steinman, and Zemmelman 1988). Gunnoe and Braver (2001), who controlled for self-selection factors, also found that, compared with sole custody families, children in joint custody families had better adjustment and fewer adjustment problems, and this finding was not moderated by the level of pre-divorce parental conflict.

More recent studies comparing joint custody/shared parenting and sole custody families, appearing after the publication of Bauserman's (2002) meta-analysis (Fabricius et al 2011 and 2010; Fabricius and Luecken 2007; Cashmore and Parkinson 2010; Bjarnason and Anarsson 2012 and 2010; Spruijt and Duindan 2010; Kaspiew et al 2009; Melli and Brown 2008; Campana et al 2008; Jablonska and Lindberg 2007; Breivik and Olweus 2006; Neoh and Mellor 2010; Finley and Schwartz 2007), have concluded that children in equal and shared parenting arrangements have consistently better outcomes on measures of emotional, behavioural, psychological, physical and academic well-being. Again, this has emerged as one of the most robust findings in divorce research (Nielsen 2013).

3 *Shared custody works for parents too. Inter-parental conflict decreases over time in shared custody arrangements, and increases in sole custody arrangements. Inter-parental co-operation increases over time in shared custody arrangements, and decreases in sole custody arrangements.* One of the key findings of Bauserman's (2002) meta-analysis was the unexpected pattern of decreasing parental conflict in joint custody families, and the increase of conflict over time in sole custody families. The less a parent feels threatened by the loss of her or his child and the parental role, the less the likelihood of subsequent conflict. Bauserman (2012) conducted a more in-depth meta-analytic review of research on parental conflict in physical/legal joint custody and sole custody families, concluding again that parental conflict and re-litigation were significantly lower in joint custody as opposed to sole custody families.

Another new finding in research on parenting after divorce related to inter-parental conflict is that of Fabricius et al (2010): equal and shared parenting offset the negative impact of parental conflict, and shield children from the negative effects of parental conflict. The benefits of shared parenting for children are evident in both co-operative family settings and parental conflict situations. Studies conclude that parental conflict should not be a determining factor in the amount of time children spend with their parents, unless the conflict involves a documented history of child abuse or family violence (Lamb and Kelly 2009; Fabricius et al 2010; Warshak 2011).

4 *Both US and Canadian research indicates that mothers and fathers working outside the home now spend about the same amount of time caring for their children. According to Health Canada's time budget research (Higgins and Duxbury 2002), on average each week mothers devote 11.1 hours to child care; fathers devote 10.5 hours. According to Statistics Canada (Marshall 2006), men, although still relatively less involved in family work tasks, have significantly increased their overall participation in primary child care.* Although research on child-to-parent attachment has revealed that children form primary

attachment bonds with each of their parents (Rutter 1995), until recently there has been very little evidence that fathers contribute to child care to the same degree as mothers, and popular beliefs about the division of child care activities assume primary maternal responsibility. The attachment-theory-based research is now reinforced by data from both Statistics Canada and Health Canada. Examining patterns of primary child care in the 2005 *General Social Survey*, Statistics Canada found that, on average, men aged twenty-five to fifty-four spent 1.8 hours a day on direct child care, while women spent 2.5 hours (Marshall 2006); the 2010 *General Social Survey* found that men spend an average of 1.9 hours, and women 2.9 hours a day on primary child care (Statistics Canada 2011). The Health Canada study (Higgins and Duxbury 2002), utilizing a representative sample of 31,571 Canadian workers, found that employed fathers and mothers are roughly equal partners with respect to the amount of time they devote to child care, as measured by the number of hours spent in the previous week on activities related to child care. Although this finding runs counter to popular beliefs about gender differences in the division of family labour, these data are consistent with time use data from the United States (Bianchi 2000). In her US-based research, Bianchi (2000) attributes the relative decline in maternal child care to six factors: (1) the reallocation of mothers' time to market work outside the home (child care time declines as work time increases); (2) over-estimations of maternal time with children in previous research (it was assumed that time at home was all invested in child care when in reality a large amount was devoted to household chores not involving children); (3) smaller families have reduced total time with young children; (4) more preschool children spend time in daycare and play group settings, regardless of the mother's employment status; (5) women's reallocation of their time has facilitated a relative increase in fathers' involvement in child care; and (6) technology such as cell phones has allowed parents to be "on call" without being physically present with children. Thus, as the gender difference in time spent in child care has diminished, shared parenting is emerging as the norm in American and

Canadian two-parent families. In divorced families, sole custody is no longer the dominant post-divorce custodial arrangement in Canada, as there has been a significant increase in joint custody among parents who are not involved in a legal contest over the custody of their children (Statistics Canada 2007).

Higgins and Duxbury's 2012 follow-up study, *The 2012 National Study on Balancing Work and Caregiving in Canada*, found that parents spend an average of 21.3 hours a week in child care or activities with their children, and a continuing trend of shared parental responsibility was noted in this regard.

PRESERVATION OF ATTACHMENT BONDS

Infants and Preschool Children

Infants and preschool children are the most adversely affected by the consequences of divorce, particularly through diminished parent-child relationships and exposure to parental conflict (Wallerstein and Kelly 1980). Especially when children are very young, their interactions with their parents need to be regular, spanning a range of activities and contexts, and separations need to be minimized, as parents who do not interact regularly with their infants and toddlers effectively become strangers (Lamb and Kelly 2009; Pruett et al 2003). Evenings and overnights provide opportunities for crucial social interactions and nurturing activities that "visits" cannot provide, including bathing, soothing hurts and anxieties, bedtime rituals, comforting in the middle of the night, and the reassurance and security of snuggling in the morning after awakening. These everyday activities create and maintain trust and confidence in the parents while deepening and strengthening parent-child attachments. When mothers are breastfeeding, there is sometimes maternal resistance regarding extended overnight or full-day separations. Breastfeeding is obviously one of the important contexts in which attachments are promoted, and parenting routines need to be arranged around the infant's feeding schedule. An attitude of support for breastfeeding mothers by fathers is critical.

Infants and very young children cannot tolerate lengthy separations from primary attachment figures. The loss or attenuation of important relationships may cause depression or anxiety, particularly in the first two years, when children lack the cognitive and communication skills that would enable them to cope with loss. The richer, deeper, and more secure the parent-child relationships, the better the child's adjustment, whether or not the parents live together. When both parents have been actively involved as caregivers in infants' lives, continued frequent opportunities for routine interaction with both parents is crucial after divorce (Lamb and Kelly 2009).

Stability, consistency in caregiving routines, and predictability of transitions between parents need to be optimal for infants and young children in caregiving arrangements after divorce (Pruett et al 2003). The pre-divorce parenting history is thus a key factor in determining the nature of the post-divorce parenting schedule, as infants form attachments to those who have been regularly available and have responded to the infant's needs and signals (Lamb and Kelly 2009).

Research on Father Absence

Thirty percent of children of divorce have not seen their father in the past year (Amato, Myers, and Emery 2009). Sole maternal custody often results in father absence (Kruk 2010b), and father absence plays a large role in children's problematic adjustment to the consequences of divorce. The research literature on father absence is robust, and it has now been empirically established that responsible fatherhood involvement is crucial to children's physical, psychological, and emotional well-being, and the absence of fathers in children's lives after divorce in particular has profoundly negative effects in multiple areas of children's lives. Interestingly, children growing up without regular father contact due to the death of the father do not suffer such ill effects; father absence specifically following parental divorce, a widespread social problem, is a key factor in child maladjustment.

A major impetus for writing this book was the mounting accumulation of data on the effects of father absence on children. However, it should be noted that although it is not a subject of empirical investigation to the same degree as father absence, the absence of mothers in children's lives has similar repercussions on children's well-being. In addition, although children are negatively affected by father absence, this does not imply that the patriarchal nuclear family structure is an ideal family form; children's optimal development is evident within bi-nuclear families as well as a range of non-traditional family structures. Nor does it imply that single mothers are the cause of developmental and social problems in children; the devaluation of fathers is but one manifestation of the devaluation and lack of support of parents in general, in contemporary culture. Rather, the data on father absence effects support a model of emergent fatherhood in which fathers are actively and responsibly involved in child rearing, within an egalitarian division of parenting responsibility between women and men.

The profound effects of father absence, particularly in situations in which fathers previously had an active role to play in their children's lives, cannot be overstated. A plethora of studies have revealed the importance of active father involvement in the development of children. The two major structural threats to fathers' presence in children's lives are divorce and non-marital childbearing. The absence of fathers in children's lives, particularly after divorce, is associated with a wide range of social problems: youth crime (85% of youth in prison have an absent father); poor academic performance (71% of high school dropouts do not have an active father); homelessness (90% of runaway children have an absent father); and children and youth whose fathers are absent exhibit higher levels of depression and suicide, delinquency, promiscuity and teen pregnancy, behavioural problems, and illicit and licit substance abuse (Stein et al 2009; Coley and Medeiros 2007; Rosenberg and Wilcox 2006; Crowder and Teachman 2004; Ellis et al 2003; Ringbäck Weitoft et al 2003; Jeynes 2001; Horwitz et al 2003; McMunn et al 2001; Blankenhorn 1995). Father absence through divorce is strongly associated with diminished self-concepts in children (Berg 2003; Dunlop, Burns and Bermingham 2001; Parish 1987), as children consistently report that they wish they had more contact with their fathers and feel abandoned when fathers are not involved in their lives after divorce (Fabricius 2003; Braver and O'Connell 1998; Warshak 1992). Father-absent children and youth are more likely to be victims of exploitation and abuse, and the *Journal of Ethnology and Sociobiology* recently reported that pre-schoolers not living with both of their biological parents (in either two-parent homes or in equal shared parenting situations after divorce) are forty times more likely to be sexually abused. Finally, children in father-absent families run greater mortality and morbidity risks (Ringbäck Weitoft et al 2003).

A generation of fatherhood advocates has emerged who suggest that fatherlessness is the most critical social issue of our time. In *Fatherless America*, David Blankenhorn calls the crisis of fatherless children "the most destructive trend of our generation" (Blankenhorn 1995, 1), arguing that virtually every major social pathology has been linked to fatherless children – violent crime, drug and alcohol abuse, truancy, unwed pregnancy, suicide, and mental health disorders all correlate more strongly with father-lessness than with any other factor, surpassing race and poverty. Empirical studies on father absence effects confirm most of Blankenhorn's claims. After controlling for child poverty and social class, studies found that in comparison with children who have ongoing relationships with both parents, father-absent children:

- are more likely to suffer from short- and long-term emotional and mental health problems, including poor self-esteem, anxiety, depression, impulsivity, and suicide (Meltzer at al 2000; Hetherington and Kelly 2002; Chase-Lansdale, Cherlin, and Kiernan 1995);
- have a higher risk of physical health problems, psychosomatic health symptoms, and illness such as acute and chronic pain, diabetes, asthma, headaches, stomach aches, and feeling sick (Holmes 2007; O'Neill 2002; Lundbert 1993; Dawson

1991), are more likely to die as children (Lundbert 1993), and live an average of four years less over their life span (Ringbäck Weitoft et al 2003; Tucker at al 1997);

- are more likely to experience problems with sexual health, including a greater likelihood of having intercourse before the age of sixteen, foregoing contraception during first intercourse, and becoming teenage parents (Ellis et al 2003; O'Neill 2002; Wellings et al 1994; Kiernan 1997), and contracting sexually transmitted infections (Wellings, Nanchanahal, and MacDowall 2001);
- are at greater risk of suffering physical, emotional, and sexual abuse; are five times more likely to have experienced physical abuse and emotional maltreatment (Cawson 2002); and are exposed to a one hundred times higher risk of fatal abuse (Daly and Wilson 1988);
- have more difficulties with behaviour and social adjustment, are more likely to report problems with friendships, experience behaviour problems and manifest antisocial and criminal behaviour (King and Soboleski 2006; McMunn et al 2001; Crowder and Teachman 2004; O'Neill 2002);
- have more trouble in school, scoring poorly on tests of reading, mathematics, and thinking skills (Menning 2006; Elliot and Richards 1985; Jeynes 2001; Horwitz et al 2003);
- are more likely to run away from home (Rees and Rutherford 2001);
- are more likely to offend and go to jail as adults (O'Neill 2002; Flood-Page et al 2000);
- are more likely to smoke, drink alcohol, and abuse drugs in childhood (Power, Rodgers and Hope 1999; Ely et al 2000; Sweeting, West and Richards 1998) and adulthood (Hope, Power, and Rodgers 1998);
- are more likely to play truant from school (Graham and Bowling 1995);
- are more likely to be excluded from school (Sweeting, West, and Richards 1998);
- are more likely to leave school at age sixteen (Ely et al 2000; Jeynes 2000);

- are less likely to attain academic and professional qualifications in adulthood (Sweeting, West, and Richards 1998; Ely et al 2000);
- are more likely to experience unemployment, have low incomes, and remain on social assistance (O'Neill 2002; Kiernan 1997);
- are more likely to experience homelessness in adulthood (Kiernan 1997);
- tend to enter partnerships earlier, are more likely to divorce or dissolve their cohabiting unions, and are more likely to have children outside marriage or outside any partnership (Kiernan 1997).

Most of these studies examined father absence in general but suggest that father absence following divorce is particularly problematic in its short- and long-term effects on children. Increasingly, however, studies have focused exclusively on father absence after divorce, isolating the effects on child well-being. Parish (1987) studied the impact of father absence after divorce and concluded that father loss was associated with difficulties in children's school-based, social, and personal adjustment, and diminished self-concept. Bisnaire, Firestone, and Rynard (1990) found a marked decrease in the post-divorce academic performance of 30% of the children with absent fathers following divorce, and this was evident three years after the divorce; access to both parents after divorce seemed to be the most protective factor in academic performance, with father involvement being most influential in children's development. Drill (1986) found that when the non-custodial father is perceived as "lost" following parental divorce, children are more likely to be depressed, and their perception of the non-custodial father changes in a negative manner. She also concluded that arrangements in which both parents are equally involved with the child after divorce are optimal. Fabricius and Luecken (2007) examined young adults' relationships with fathers after divorce and found that poor father-child relationships and more distress associated with ongoing parental conflict predicted children's poorer health status after parental divorce, and that more time with fathers was beneficial for children in both high- and low-conflict families. Amato and Gilbreth's (1999) meta-analysis of sixty-three studies examining the relationship between the frequency of father contact after divorce and child outcomes concluded with the recommendation that child custody laws and policies be changed so that fathers are not restricted to weekend time with their children. In a more recent review of research, Amato and Dorius (2012, 192) again conclude that "policies and interventions designed to improve ties between fathers and children should be maintained and encouraged."

Several studies have examined the impact of father absence following divorce on girls in particular. Frost and Pakiz (1990) found that girls from father-absent divorced families become more involved with alcohol or drugs, reported skipping school and higher levels of depression, and described social support in more negative terms than girls from father-involved families. Legg, Mendell, and Riemer (1989) found that particular coping patterns among girls emerge in response to the absence of the father, observable during the latency years, including intensified separation anxiety, denial and avoidance of feelings associated with the loss of the father, identification with the lost object, and object hunger for males. The three most commonly occurring problems were psychological distress (defined as anxiety, sadness, pronounced moodiness, phobias, and depression, affecting 69% of the sample), academic problems, and performance substantially below one's ability or past performance (affecting 47%), and aggression toward parents (affecting 41%). Finally, Kalter (1987) found that among teenage and adult populations of females, father absence following parental divorce was associated with lower self-esteem, precocious sexual activity, greater delinquent-like behaviour, and more difficulty establishing gratifying, lasting adult heterosexual relationships; in these cases parental divorce typically occurred years before any difficulties were observed. He noted:

> At the time of the marital separation, when (as is typical) the father leaves the family home and becomes progressively less involved with his children over the ensuing years, it appears

that young girls experience the emotional loss of father ego-centrically as a rejection of them. While more common among preschool and early elementary school girls, we have observed this phenomenon clinically in later elementary school and young adolescent children. Here children experience the continued lack of involvement of the father as an ongoing rejection by him. Many girls attribute this rejection to their not being pretty enough, affectionate enough, athletic enough, or smart enough to please the father and engage him in regular, frequent contact. Girls whose parents divorce may grow up without the day-to-day experience of interacting with a man who is attentive, caring and loving ... Without this regular source of nourishment, a girl's sense of being valued as a female does not seem to thrive.

In general, however, boys seem to pay a higher price than girls when they have little or no relationship with their fathers after divorce. Boys in father-absent families are more socially immature, aggressive, delinquent, defiant, and psychologically or emotionally disturbed than other boys their age, and suffer the effects of father absence in the long term (Warshak 1992; Buchanan, Maccoby, and Dornbusch 1996; Biller 1993; Corneau 1991; Emery 1994; Chase-Lansdale, Cherlin, and Kiernan 1995; Wallerstein 1991). Sons are also more affected by a mother's negative opinions of her former spouse, which can do more harm to him than the lack of contact with his father (Warshak 1992). Boys are more likely than girls to become enmeshed with their mothers in ways that hurt their relationships with their fathers (Corneau 1991; Emery 1994; Wallerstein 1991). Sons also seem to be especially affected by a divorced mother's moods, depression, and conflicts with fathers (Capaldi, Forgatch, and Crosby 1994; Emery 1994; Wallerstein 1991).

PRESERVATION OF PARENT-CHILD RELATIONSHIPS VIA SHARED AND EQUAL PARENTING

Sole custody and primary residence orders are highly correlated with parental disengagement after divorce, particularly father absence (Kruk 2010a; Kruk 2010b; Amato, Myers, and Emery 2009). Traditional visiting patterns and guidelines are, for the majority of children, outdated, unnecessarily rigid, and restrictive, and fail in both the short and long term to address their best interests (Kelly 2007). Before and after divorce, children need both parents actively involved in their lives for their optimal development, and the removal of a primary parent threatens their physical and emotional security. Numerous studies (Campana et al 2008; Melli and Brown 2008; Gunnoe and Braver 2001; Laumann-Billings and Emery 2000; Amato and Gilbreth 1999; Lamb 1999; Lamb, Sternberg, and Thompson 1997; Buchanan, Maccoby, and Dornbusch 1996; Bender 1994; Warshak 1992; Bisnaire, Firestone, and Rynard 1990) have demonstrated the salutary effects of equal and shared parenting, and joint physical custody, compared to sole custody, on children's divorce-specific and general adjustment; Kelly (2000), in reviewing a decade of research on child outcomes, concluded that joint custody led to significantly better child outcomes. Finally, Bauserman's (2002) meta-analysis of thirty-three major North American studies comparing child and parent outcomes in joint versus sole custody homes, and his 2012 meta-analysis of fifty studies from 2002 to 2012 comparing parent outcomes in joint versus sole custody homes (including major peer-reviewed studies and PhD dissertations on the subject), and both self-selected samples and those with legally mandated joint-physical-custody arrangements found that joint custody is associated with more salutary outcomes for children and parents. Comparing child adjustment in joint-physical-custody and legal custody settings with sole custody, as well as intact family settings, and examining children's general adjustment, family relationships, self-esteem, emotional and behavioural adjustment, divorce-specific adjustment, as well as the degree and nature of ongoing conflict between parents, Bauserman found that children in joint custody arrangements fare significantly better than those in sole custody on all measures. High conflict families fared as well as the self-selected samples, reinforcing the findings of earlier studies that joint custody works equally well for high conflict families in which parents are vying for custody (Benjamin and Irving 1989; Brotsky, Steinman, and Zemmelman 1988).

Given the plethora of empirical research supporting equal and shared parenting, we are now at a point where we can substitute the theoretical and ideological debates surrounding parenting after divorce with a more concrete and practical approach based on empirical research findings. The research summarized above provides sufficiently robust statistical inferences to allow valid conclusions to be drawn, and these conclusions are unequivocally favourable to equal and shared parenting responsibility.

6

High Conflict, Family Violence, and Parenting after Divorce

Given the fact that inter-parental conflict is a key factor affecting children's adjustment to divorce, it is not surprising that family violence is an integral issue in the parenting after divorce debate. Although it is generally agreed that unresolved, protracted high conflict between parents is harmful to children's well-being, the position that equal or shared parenting is not in children's best interests in cases in which parents are in conflict over post-divorce parenting arrangements is not supported by research (Fabricius et al 2011). And although there is general agreement that equal or shared parenting may be contraindicated in cases of proven violence and abuse, either toward a child or a parent as the witnessing of parental abuse is a form of child abuse (Kitzmann et al 2003; Trocme et al 2005), few would suggest that a mere allegation of abuse on the part of a parent should be sufficient to deny the other parent access to his or her children, or to accept a parent's allegations at face value. False allegations of abuse are prevalent in child custody disputes, as spouses in high conflict divorces routinely make false or exaggerated allegations in an attempt to gain a tactical advantage in the custody contest (Birnbaum and Bala 2010; Allen and Brinig 2011). Legal scholars assert that family violence should be considered a serious criminal matter (Chisolm 2009) and increasingly it is being recognized that false allegations of violence should also be seen as a form of legal abuse of a parent (Brown 2004). A zero-tolerance policy

with respect to inter-parental violence and child abuse is fundamental in the process of legal determination of parenting after
divorce; also, however, false allegations which, when proven false,
trivialize the very real problem of spousal abuse, must also be
addressed by means of zero tolerance.

High conflict is almost universal in contested child custody
disputes (Dutton 2005a), and there is at times a fine line between
"normal" family conflict and abuse. Surprisingly, few scholars
have differentiated among different types of high conflict and
abuse in the arena of parenting after divorce, although there are
some beginning attempts in this regard (Birnbaum and Bala 2010;
Johnston and Campbell 1993; Johnson 2005). Most child and
family scholars and practitioners view family violence as a serious
criminal matter, which must be treated as such; a criminal conviction of assault against a spouse or a finding that a child is in need
of protection from a parent should be sufficient to deny a parent
equal or shared parenting. An unproven allegation of abuse, however, even in the context of a high conflict divorce, is not grounds
to withdraw parenting responsibilities from a parent, as the routine involvement of both parents is important to the well-being
of children.

GENERAL FAMILY VIOLENCE RESEARCH

Family violence and abuse after divorce are set in the context of
family violence in general. A high proportion of first-time family
violence (usually of a reciprocal nature) occurs after divorce. In
most of the popular family violence literature, men are repre-
sented as primary perpetrators of physical abuse and women
almost always as the victims; however, research data utilizing
nationally representative data sets and meta-analytic analyses
indicate otherwise. A meta-analytic review of family violence
research of 250 empirical studies (Fiebert 2004) concludes that
women and men perpetrate and receive abuse at comparable levels; women are as physically aggressive as men in their relationships with their spouses or male partners. Archer's (2002 and
2000) meta-analytic reviews found that women are more likely

than men to use aggression toward their heterosexual partners, and more likely to be injured by them. Archer describes an overlooked norm: that men should restrain themselves from physical aggression towards women, even when women are themselves assaultive. Data from the US National Family Violence Survey, reported by Stets and Straus (1990), showed that 28.6% of married couples experiencing family violence were female violent (with a non-violent male), and 48.2% were physically mutually abusive. Whitaker et al (2007) also found that half of all partner violence is reciprocal. There is, however, a trend of increasing female-to-male violence being noted. Whitaker et al (2007) found that in non-reciprocally violent relationships, women were the perpetrators in more than 70% of cases. Hampton, Gelles, and Harrop (1989) report steady rates of male to female violence, but an increase of 33% in female to male violence over a ten-year period.

The fact that female-to-male violence has been overlooked has been a concern to family violence researchers: Stets and Henderson (1991) found that women were six times more likely than men to use severe violence in dating relationships and inflict more severe violence in cohabiting and married relationships; Stets and Straus (1992) and Straus (1995) found that violence by women is not primarily defensive, yet is less disapproved of than male-to-female violence. Female initiation of partner violence is the leading reason for a woman becoming a victim of violence herself (Stith et al 2004). McNeely, Cook, and Torres (2001, 227) conclude that domestic violence is a human, not gender-specific, issue, as women are as violent as men in domestic relationships, and comment specifically on men's "legal and social defenselessness."

Canadian data show similar patterns. According to Statistics Canada's (2008) analysis of Canadian Centre for Justice Statistics data, in a national sample, 8% of women and 7% of men reported abuse by their intimate partners over the previous five-year period. Of these, 23% of women and 15% of men suffered severe violence. The nature, severity, and consequences of violence are similar, but 33% of men and 66% of women report being injured.

The US Center for Disease Control's central finding in its National Intimate Partner and Sexual Violence Survey (Black et al 2011) is that men and women inflict and suffer equal rates of interpersonal violence, with 6.5% of men and 6.3% of women experiencing partner aggression in the past year. Other Canadian data indicate that there is twice as much wife-to-husband as husband-to-wife severe violence (Brinkerhoff and Lupri 1988; Sommer 1994). In regard to homicides, however, more women are victimized; in 2008, there were sixty-two spousal homicides in Canada, and forty-five of these were female victims (Statistics Canada 2008).

Johnson (2005) points out that while domestic violence rates between men and women in intimate relationships are similar, it is important to distinguish between levels of severity, and that of the three types of partner violence – situational couple violence (the most common type), violent resistance, and intimate terrorism (the type most likely to be ongoing and brutal) – intimate terrorism is most likely to be injurious and ongoing. A wide range of studies (Ehrensaft, Moffitt, and Caspi 2004; Moffitt et al 2001; Dutton 2006a) indicate that this type of intimate partner violence is relatively rare; violence at this degree of severity occurs in only 2 to 4% of the cases of domestic abuse to which police respond (Statistics Canada 2008; Brown 2004), and the great majority of such domestic violence is bilateral (Dutton 2005a), although others (Johnson 2005) argue that violence is primarily male-perpetrated and best understood through a feminist theory of domestic violence. Contrary to Johnson's assertions about higher rates of intimate terrorism by males, Stets and Straus's (1992) US-based national survey data indicated that "unilateral severe violence" against non-violent partners was three times as common for female perpetrators as for male perpetrators. Archer's (2002 and 2000) meta-analytic finding was that there were minor differences in violence and injuries by gender. From the Canadian General Social Survey, Laroche (2005) found a rate of 2% female intimate terrorists compared to 3% male intimate terrorists.

When police respond to cases of domestic abuse, men are treated more harshly by the law-enforcement system at every step of the process, with the disparity most noticeable in cases in which Statistics Canada reports the greatest equality in perpetration, low-level disputes in which neither party suffered any injury. In this category of cases, men are nineteen times more likely to be charged than women (Brown 2004); men are more likely to be criminally charged even when they report that their partners have abused them, and thus men are less likely to report abuse than women (Brown 2004; Straus 1999). Men are only one-tenth as likely as women to call police when assaulted, and are far more likely to be arrested when they initiate police contact (Brown 2004; Stets and Straus 1992) because police refuse to take violence against men seriously (Buzawa et al 1992; Brown 2004). Criminal justice statistics of family violence thus reflect systemic biases in the way police handle and subsequently record domestic violence.

Dutton (2005a) examined the disparity between the results of national survey data and meta-analytic research on family violence, and popular assumptions about family violence, which are also supported by research, although based entirely on police reports or clinical agency-based samples. Jaffe, Lemon, and Poisson (2003, 6), for example, conclude that, "women are four times more likely to experience the most serious and potentially lethal violence, such as threats, assault with a gun or knife, choking, or sexual assault ... and three times more likely to report suffering a physical injury and twice as likely to report chronic ongoing assaults"; and Dutton (2005a, 32) cites Sudermann and Jaffe (1998) as claiming that "the overwhelming majority of instances of marital violence involve women as victims and men as perpetrators." The discrepancy between the findings of meta-analytic investigations and studies that report that women are disproportionately the victims of severe violence is striking. Dutton (2005a) offers this explanation: almost without exception, the research based upon studies utilizing a "gender paradigm" explanation of domestic violence uses samples drawn from battered women's shelters or treatment groups for men who batter, which are then generalized. Surveys that ask only women about their victimization are common (Dutton 2010); the

Canadian Violence against Women Survey is one example. As Magdol et al (1997, 68) point out, "the expectation that rates of partner violence by men would exceed rates by women stem from the sampling choices of previous studies." Research based on self-selected samples of extreme cases is highly problematic, as research conducted in women's shelters is typically vetted by feminist directives that preclude asking questions about women's role in the violence, as this is considered to be a form of "victim blaming" (Dutton 2005b). Dutton notes that research utilizing such self-selected and non-representative samples creates a distorted and potentially harmful perception, perpetuating the stereotype that only men are violent in the family and that only women are victims of violence. This stereotype has had a strong effect on the legal determination of parenting after divorce in Canadian courts (ibid).

As a result of the gender paradigm characterizing family violence research based largely on non-representative agency samples, there is now strong evidence of a pervasive anti-male bias in the justice system; since 1984, over 1,000 studies have been conducted by the federal and provincial governments on the incidences and effects of women's victimization (Dutton 2005a); only a handful have examined men as victims (Lupri and Grandin 2004).

Apart from interpersonal violence directed toward a partner, there also exists, in the dominant gender paradigm discourse about male violence against women and children, erroneous information about child abuse. A key source of data on child abuse in Canada is the *Canadian Incidence Study of Reported Child Abuse and Neglect 2003* (Trocme et al 2005), which indicates that fathers and mothers about equally perpetrate the abuse of children, although mothers pose a slightly greater risk to children, with boys more frequently abused than girls. Again, although it is often assumed that fathers are the primary perpetrators of abuse, mothers are the more likely substantiated perpetrator of physical abuse (in 47% versus 42% of all cases of abuse), neglect (86% versus 33%), emotional maltreatment (61% versus 55%), and other categories (66% versus 55%), except sexual abuse, in which more fathers than mothers are found to be perpetrators (15% versus 5%). Unsubstantiated allegations of child abuse are also commonplace in the context of child custody disputes (Kruk 2010a).

PARENTING-AFTER-DIVORCE-SPECIFIC FAMILY VIOLENCE RESEARCH

Despite the strong evidence that family violence is committed by both genders at the same frequency and with about equal consequences (Laroche 2005; Pimlott-Kubiak and Cortina 2003; Serbin et al 2004), the prevailing assumption of police and the court system is that the overwhelming majority of instances of severe spousal violence involve women as victims and men as perpetrators, and that severe interpersonal violence is overwhelmingly directed by men toward women. As mentioned, this has had a profound impact on the legal determination of parenting after divorce (Dutton 2005a). Having made the assumption that family violence is primarily male-to-female-directed, Jaffe, Lemon, and Poisson (2003 and 2005) instruct judges to look at fathers as potential abuse perpetrators, and to suspect fathers' denial of abuse. One model of family violence predominates: the father is the batterer, the mother is the victim, and the child is victimized by observation of the father's violence. When abuse perpetrators are not male, the abuse is largely dismissed as either not serious or in self-defence. When the abuse is non-retaliatory, male abuse is seen as more serious. Yet, female-initiated violence is more common than assumed, and levels of severity of violence are similar between women and men, with the most common form of domestic violence being bilateral (Stets and Straus 1992).

In a wide array of family violence research, erroneous generalizing from non-representative samples also creates the perception that only men are abusers and only women are victims of violence, and this has become enshrined in child custody policy and practice. Yet, when inter-parental conflict and violence are conceived in a one-sided manner, with attention focused solely on the possibility of abuse by a male perpetrator, actual child safety is compromised (Dutton 2005a). In the arena of child custody, most cases of high conflict involve no violence. When spousal violence does exist, it usually involves bilateral violence, and cases in which the female partner is the primary or sole instigator (Dutton 2005a; Johnston and Campbell 1993). Johnston and Campbell (1993) offer a useful typology of cases of family violence in the context of child custody / parenting disputes, including ongoing or episodic battering by men, female initiated violence, male-controlling interactive violence (with men seeking to control), separation and divorce violence, and psychotic and paranoid reactions; they conclude that mutual violence is the most common type, with male battering constituting less than one-fifth of cases of violence. Contrary to the views of proponents of the gender paradigm, not all acts of intimate partner violence have motivations and expressions derived from a male assumption of entitlement and need for control (the classic "cycle of violence" theory).

The questionable claims of gender paradigm proponents have had profound repercussions, and the biases they have generated are troublesome. According to Jaffe, Lemon, and Poisson (2003), and Jaffe, Crooks, and Bala (2005), false denials by (male) abusers are more common than false allegations by (female) alleged victims, and the act of fathers petitioning the courts for joint custody is often an attempt of males to continue their dominance over females. Jaffe, Lemon and Poisson (2003, 18) contend that "many batterers pursue visitation as a way of getting access to their ex-partners. They may seek custody to engage in prolonged litigation, during which their legal counsel and the court process mirrors the dynamics of the abusive relationship." Neither claim is supported empirically. Relatively few contested child custody cases involve substantiated cases of child abuse, including the child witnessing abuse of a parent; only one-quarter of all child abuse allegations are substantiated after investigation (Trocme et al 2005). Yet, the incidence of violence is elevated after separation and divorce; 28% of separated women and 22% of men experience some type of violence by their partners in the previous five-year period, while living together or after separation (Hotton 2001). The threat of losing one's children in a custody contest exacerbates and creates violence, as 40 to 46% of first-time violence occurs after separation and divorce, within the winner-take-all sole custody system (Ellis and Wight-Peasley 1986; Hotton 2003; Johnson and Hotton 2003; Statistics Canada 2008). Statistics Canada's General Social Survey data indicate that whereas in most cases in which there has been violence during cohabitation, conflict and violence decrease after divorce with sole custody, in non-violence cases sole custody determinations are associated with increased conflict and first-time violence (Spiwak and Brownridge 2005). Thus, of great concern is the assertion of Jaffe, Lemon, and Poisson (2003, 15) that "an essential principle from the high-conflict divorce arena is that joint custody and shared parenting are not viable resolutions." In fact, shared parenting and joint physical custody are associated with lower inter-parental conflict levels than sole custody, even in court-determined joint custody and shared residence (Bauserman 2002 and 2012), as a high-conflict case not involving violence has a much higher likelihood of escalating to violence when one's relationship with one's child is threatened by loss of custody. The sole custody regime elevates the risk of spousal abuse and the number of children witnessing the abuse.

Jaffe, Lemon, and Poisson (2003) do not discuss the application of the child-in-need-of-protection standard to divorced families, as it is applied for non-divorced families, although they suggest a comprehensive child welfare assessment in alleged cases of family violence in which child custody is at issue. If the child-in-need-of-protection standard were to be applied in a consistent fashion, the problem of violence in custody cases would be addressed by means of investigations by trained professionals; without it, the current sole custody/primary residence framework will continue to increase the likelihood of violence in families with no previous abuse. There is no debate that judicial determination of custody in cases of established family violence is needed; it is erroneous, however, to assume that high conflict cases, in which parents disagree on custodial arrangements for children after divorce, commonly involve serious family violence. This places children at risk of losing one of their parents via a sole custody or primary residence order, and increases the risk of family violence in the majority of contested custody cases that did not previously involve violence.

Finally, suicide rates are reported to be of epidemic proportions among separated and divorced fathers struggling to maintain a parenting relationship with their children (Kposowa 2000); and legal abuse has been noted in non-custodial father suicide cases (Kposowa 2003). Studies are just beginning to examine the impact of legal abuse – that is, using a legal advantage to remove a parent from a child's life via sole custody, and subsequent parental alienation. Uprooting children in this manner and alienating the parent is itself a form of child abuse, yet often ignored (see chapter 9).

In sum, in cases of family violence in which there is a criminal conviction or a finding that a child is in need of protection from a parent, it may be appropriate, as Jaffe, Crooks, and Bala (2005) recommend, for one parent to have more limited, supervised, or no contact with children because of potential harm to the children and the spouse. In the absence of such a finding, however, sole custody and primary residence orders clearly pose serious risks to children and parents; sole custody in cases in which family violence and child abuse are not present is a flawed and dangerous policy which has markedly increased the risk of post-divorce violence in families with no previous history of violence. In the absence of investigation and clear determination of abuse and violence by the criminal court or child protective services, the family court should not assume the role of adjudicating conflicting allegations of abuse by the two parents. The majority of high-conflict child custody cases do not involve family violence, although a high proportion do involve unsubstantiated allegations of violence and abuse (Millar 2010). These should be dealt with in criminal court in the case of spousal abuse, and by child protective services in cases in which it is alleged that a child is in need of protection from a parent. While parents with a proven history of severe violence will need different resolutions, the majority of litigating parents in conflict over the care and custody of their children are best served, in the interests of prevention of severe violence, by an equal or shared parenting approach to child custody.

REDUCTION OF PARENTAL CONFLICT AND
PREVENTION OF FAMILY VIOLENCE

There is no question that exposure to ongoing and unresolved high conflict is harmful to children. What is under debate is the amount of parenting time that is advisable in high conflict situations. Research has produced mixed findings on this question, as studies have rarely distinguished between frequency of contact and actual parenting time. Earlier research (Johnston, Kline, and Tschann 1989) examined frequency of parent-child contact, and found negative outcomes in cases involving high conflict and frequent alternations between mothers' and fathers' homes. Kelly (2007), however, notes that the amount of shared parenting time is not as problematic for children as the frequency of contact in high conflict situations, and suggests limiting frequency of alternations and arranging for transitions with no direct parental contact. More recent studies have examined parenting time, as opposed to frequency of contact, and have found that equal and shared parenting not only are not harmful in high conflict situations, but also can ameliorate the harmful effects of high conflict: a warm relationship with both parents is a protective factor for children in high conflict families (Lamb and Kelly 2009; Fabricius et al 2010). Thus, Pruett et al (2003) concluded that the effects of parental conflict on child outcomes are mediated by paternal involvement; Gunnoe and Braver (2001) and Bauserman (2002) found that the benefits of joint custody on children's well-being exist independent of parental conflict; and Fabricius and Luecken (2007) concluded that shared parenting is beneficial for children in both low and high conflict situations. Children are able to have warm and supportive relationships with parents who have highly conflicted relationships with each other.

Toews and McKenry (2001), examining predictors of parental co-operation and conflict after divorce in a survey of 237 divorced parents, found that joint custody was positively related to parental co-operation. Theirs is among a number of studies examined in Bauserman's (2002) meta-analysis (see chapter 5); Bauserman concluded, comparing parental outcomes in joint versus sole custody families, that joint custody is associated with a significant reduction of parental conflict levels.

At the same time, winner-take-all adversarial processes and sole custody or primary residence orders are strongly associated with exacerbation or creation of parental conflict. Parental conflict is highest during the divorce transition, in the context of disputed child custody. Hawthorne and Lennings (2008) found that limiting fathers' involvement in children's lives via sole maternal custody judgments was correlated with their reported level of subsequent hostility toward their ex-wives. Inter-parental conflict decreases over time in shared custody arrangements, and increases in sole custody arrangements; inter-parental co-operation increases over time in shared custody arrangements, and decreases in sole custody arrangements (Bauserman 2002 and 2012; Melli and Brown 2008). Fully half of first-time family violence occurs after divorce, within the context of the adversarial winner-take-all sole custody system (Ellis and Wight-Peasley 1986; Hotton 2003; Johnson and Hotton 2003; Statistics Canada 2008).

There is no evidence to support the contention that equal or shared parental responsibility increases inter-parental conflict (Bauserman 2002; Gunnoe and Braver 2001). The research does not support a presumption that the amount of parenting time should be limited in cases of high conflict, and high conflict should not be used to justify restrictions on children's contact with either of their parents (Lamb and Kelly 2009; Fabricius and Luecken 2007). Currently, mere allegations of conflict and violence are powerful tools in the adversarial sole custody system, frequently resulting in the reduction of contact between children and parents so accused (Sternberg 1997). As will be argued in chapter 7, equal and shared parenting are associated with reduction of conflict and increased parental co-operation, and as the adjustment of children to divorce is highly contingent upon these factors, an equal-parental-responsibility presumption is preventive of ongoing conflict and first-time violence after divorce, and thus contributory to children's long-term well-being.

7

Sixteen Arguments in Support
of Equal Parenting

The case for equal parenting presented below is based upon the research literature discussed in chapters 5 and 6. Given this data and the drawbacks of the best-interests-of-the-child standard and the harms attendant to the sole custody/primary residence model detailed in chapter 4, each of the sixteen arguments that follow may be sufficient reason to adopt equal parenting as a viable alternative to the sole custody/primary residence approach; combined, they are a powerful testament to the urgent need for law reform in the direction of an equal parenting presumption. Recent research studies cited in support of each argument have utilized larger and more representative samples than previous studies, overcoming most of the methodological limitations of earlier research.

The sixteen arguments in support of equal parenting are as follows:

1 Equal parenting preserves children's relationships with both parents.
2 Equal parenting preserves parents' relationships with their children.
3 Equal parenting decreases parental conflict and prevents family violence.
4 Equal parenting reflects children's preferences and views about their needs and best interests.

5 Equal parenting reflects parents' preferences and views about their children's needs and best interests.

6 Equal parenting reflects child caregiving arrangements before divorce.

7 Equal parenting enhances the quality of parent-child relationships.

8 Equal parenting decreases parental focus on "mathematizing time" and reduces litigation.

9 Equal parenting provides an incentive for inter-parental negotiation, mediation, and the development of co-operative parenting plans.

10 Equal parenting provides a clear and consistent guideline for judicial decision-making.

11 Equal parenting reduces the risk and incidence of parental alienation.

12 Equal parenting enables enforcement of parenting orders, as parents are more likely to abide by an equal parenting order.

13 Equal parenting addresses social justice imperatives regarding protection of children's rights.

14 Equal parenting addresses social justice imperatives regarding parental authority, autonomy, equality, rights, and responsibilities.

15 The discretionary best-interests-of-the-child/sole custody model is not empirically supported.

16 A rebuttable legal presumption of equal parenting responsibility is empirically supported.

1 Equal parenting preserves children's relationships with both parents. As detailed in chapter 5, equal parenting preserves children's relationships with both parents, and this is critical to children's adjustment to divorce. It has long been established that both before and after divorce, for optimal development, children need both of their parents to be physically and emotionally attuned, involved, and responsive in their lives, and the removal of a primary parent threatens their physical and emotional security. Maccoby and Mnookin (1992), in the landmark Stanford Custody Project, in which data was collected over a four-year period from 1,100 divorced families with 1,386 children, found that four years after divorce, dual residence children were better off academically, emotionally, and psychologically than children in sole custody arrangements. Lund (1987), in a qualitative study comparing post-divorce child outcomes in harmonious co-parent, conflicted co-parent, and father-absent families, found that the benefits of co-parenting were evident in both the harmonious and conflicted co-parenting groups, and that the strongest predictor of child well-being was the active involvement of co-parents in children's lives. More recent studies (Campana et al 2008; Melli and Brown 2008; Gunnoe and Braver 2001; and others cited in chapter 5) have demonstrated the salutary effects of joint physical custody (compared to sole custody) on children's divorce-specific and general adjustment; Fabricius et al (2011) concluded that children's highest level of emotional security is achieved through 50% time spent with each of their parents, and confirmed the findings of Sandler, Cookston, and Braver (2008), that shared parenting arrangements shield children from the effects of parental conflict. Melli and Brown (2008) found that children in shared parenting families were less depressed, exhibited fewer health problems and health-related illnesses, felt more life satisfaction than children in sole custody families, and were less likely to have been left with babysitters and in daycare. Jablonska and Lindberg (2007), in a Swedish study of 15,428 children, found that shared parenting children ran no increased risk of negative outcomes after divorce, as opposed to children in sole parenting homes. Breivik and Olweus's 2006 Norwegian study found that children in shared parenting arrangements had higher self-esteem, less depression, less substance abuse, and less anti-social behaviour than children in primary residence families. Bjarnason's 2010 and 2012 comparative studies of 200,000 children in thirty-six countries found that children in equal and shared parenting had significantly higher levels of life satisfaction and contentment, and enjoyed more positive relationships with their parents than children in other post-divorce arrangements. In fact, three quarters of the children in equal and shared parenting families ranked their level of life satisfaction as equivalent to or higher than children in two-parent families. Finally, as detailed in chapter 5, Bauserman's (2002) meta-analysis of studies comparing child and parent outcomes in sole and joint custody families, and (2012) meta-analysis of studies comparing parent outcomes, found that joint custody and shared parenting resulted in significantly better outcomes for children and parents on all divorce-specific and general measures of adjustment, including children's family relationships, self-esteem, and emotional and behavioural adjustment, and the level of ongoing conflict between parents. High conflict families with court-determined arrangements fared as well as those voluntarily opting for equal and shared parenting, reinforcing the findings of earlier studies that joint custody works equally well for high conflict families in which parents are vying for custody (Buchanan, Maccoby, and Dornbush 1996; Crosbie-Burnett 1991; Healy, Malley, and Stewart 1990).

Traditional visiting patterns and guidelines are, for the majority of children, outdated, unnecessarily rigid, restrictive, artificial, and unfulfilling, and fail in both the short and long term to address their best interests (Kelly 2007). In addition, sole custody and primary residence orders are highly correlated with parental alienation and disengagement (Kruk 2010a; Kruk 2010b; Amato, Meyers, and Emery 2009); and a multitude of studies have demonstrated that father absence, particularly after divorce, more than any other single factor, is associated with children's compromised social and emotional well-being. Inasmuch as the winner-take-all sole custody approach removes a primary caregiver from children's lives, robbing children of the love of one of their parents and uprooting them from their extended family, cultural roots, and traditions, an alternative approach is urgently needed. An equal-parental-responsibility presumption preserves children's relationships with both parents.

Equal parenting arrangements are durable over the long term and provide significantly more and better quality parental care time for children than sole custody arrangements, in which children spend 30% more time in substitute care (Melli and Brown

2008; Lamb and Kelly 2009). An equal-parental-responsibility presumption maximizes the available resources of both parents for the betterment of the child.

Infants and young children are the most adversely affected by the consequences of parental divorce, particularly the absence of a primary attachment figure in their lives, especially when both parents were actively involved before divorce. Research from an attachment theory perspective (Lamb and Kelly 2009; Pruett et al 2003) confirms that infants and toddlers need regular interaction with each of their parents as attachment figures, as relationships with both mothers and fathers are psychologically important. The loss or attenuation of either of these relationships will cause depression and anxiety. Evening and overnight periods with both parents are psychologically important as they provide opportunities for crucial social interactions and nurturing activities. Transitions that are more frequent are needed for children of this age to ensure continuity of both relationships and to promote children's security and comfort. In sum, equal parenting results in an increase in the level and quality of parental stimulation and attention in children's lives after divorce, a critical factor in children's adjustment to the consequences of divorce, whereas traditional access leads to the attenuation of parent-child relationships.

2 *Equal parenting preserves parents' relationships with their children.* Just as children need both parents, so parents need their children in their lives. Studies have demonstrated that equal parenting has salutary effects on parents, as well as a positive enhancement of parental adjustment to the consequences of divorce (Bauserman 2002 and 2012; Melli and Brown 2008; Neoh and Mellor 2010). Primary among the benefits for parents with equal parental responsibility are better physical and emotional health, and less stress, resulting from the sense of purpose and personal gratification associated with active parenting; the highest levels of depression occur among adults who have a child under the age of eighteen with whom they are not living or actively involved (Neoh and Mellor 2010; Evenson

and Simon 2005). The most salient loss for parents in the divorce transition is that of their children and their parental identity (Kruk 2010a; Kruk 2010b). The constraints of the traditional access relationship following divorce are strongly associated with contact loss (ibid), as 30% of children of divorce have no contact with their non-residential fathers (Amato, Meyers, and Emery 2009). At the same time, the number of non-residential mothers is increasing, and they experience similar adjustment problems associated with the absence of their children (Kruk 2010b).

Twenty years ago, I found that parents who lost contact with their children following divorce suffered a grief reaction containing all the major elements of a bereavement (Kruk 1991). Today these parents are manifesting an even more pronounced reaction of post-traumatic stress, as they are acutely aware of the consequences of their absence in their children's lives. The loss of one's children and the parent role is a defining and organizing experience that forms the core of non-resident parents' post-divorce identity. These parents routinely report increasing isolation, loss of employment, and inability to form or sustain new relationships, and these impacts are connected to more disturbed patterns of thinking and feelings, including shame, stigma, self-blame, and learned helplessness and hopelessness about the future (Kruk 2010a; Kruk 2010b). As mentioned, a suicide epidemic has been identified among divorced fathers without custody, linked directly to family court judgments that remove them as routine caregivers of their children (Kposowa 2000).

An equal-parental-responsibility presumption would go a long way toward preventing parental disengagement from children's lives in situations in which parents want to maintain an active role as caregivers to their children, but are prevented or constrained from doing so by custody orders that remove them as primary caregivers. The fact that these parents want to live with their children and seek at least a shared care arrangement is a reflection of their attachment to their children (Kruk 2010a; Kruk 1993b). Contrary to the claims of equal parental responsibility opponents (Jaffe, Lemon, and Poisson 2003), there is no evidence that parents who seek custody of their children are doing so for reasons such as avoidance or reduction of child support payments, leverage in property settlement, or to continue their domination over their former spouses (Maccoby and Mnookin 1992). Most parents have strong primary attachments to their children and seek custodial arrangements that will enable them to maintain these attachments; feeling important and competent as a parent, being actively involved with children on a routine basis, and maintaining a relationship with one's children without interference from the other parent or other outside sources are identified by parents as key elements in the post-divorce parent-child relationship (Tepp 1983; Kaspiew et al 2009).

Whereas non-resident parents suffer the acute effects of child absence, custodial parents are typically overwhelmed by sole responsibility for their children's care, and diminished parenting results, as parents are less physically and emotionally available to their children (Lamb and Kelly 2009; Kelly 2007; Kelly 2003). Maximizing parental well-being encourages and increases parental availability and responsiveness to children, and this in turn maximizes children's well-being. Children's well-being is compromised when a parent is relegated to "second-class" status; if a parent is diminished in the eyes of a child, the child's self-esteem suffers (Kruk 2010a). Parents should be the pride of their children. Finally, sole custody outcomes reinforce women's traditional economic dependence on men, whereas an equal-parental-responsibility presumption puts pressure on governments to address wage differentials between women and men (Pulkingham 1994).

3 *Equal parenting decreases parental conflict and prevents family violence.* As Birnbaum and Bala (2010) have argued, it is essential in the legal determination of parenting after divorce to differentiate among types of high conflict. Conflict is a normal part of everyday life, and to shield children from normal conflict is doing them a disservice, whereas family violence and child abuse are dangerous to children. A rebuttable presumption of equal parental responsibility would exclude cases of violence and child abuse. Children of divorce should be afforded the same

protections as all other children when there is an investigated finding that a child is in need of protection from a parent; and family violence should be recognized in criminal law (Chisolm 2009). Family violence does not abate unless allegations are fully investigated and, where necessary, prosecuted via criminal proceedings (ibid).

There is also no question that exposure to ongoing and unresolved high conflict is harmful to children. What is under debate is the amount of parenting time that is advisable in high conflict situations. As detailed in chapter 6, research studies have rarely distinguished between frequency of contact and actual parenting time. Earlier research (Johnston, Kline, and Tschann 1989) examined frequency of contact, and found negative outcomes in cases involving high conflict and frequent visits. Kelly (2007), however, notes that the amount of shared parenting time is not as problematic for children as the frequency of contact in high conflict situations, and suggests limiting frequency of alternations and arranging for transitions with no direct parental contact. More recent studies have examined the actual amount of parenting time, as opposed to frequency of contact, and have found not only that equal and shared parental responsibility is not harmful in high conflict situations, but equal and shared parenting can ameliorate the harmful effects of high conflict: a warm relationship with both parents is a protective factor for children in high conflict families. The benefits of equal and shared parenting on children's well-being exist independent of parental conflict. As discussed in chapter 6, Pruett et al (2003) found that that the negative consequences of parental conflict on child well-being are diminished by the active involvement of both parents in children's lives; and Sandler et al (2008), Gunnoe and Braver (2001) and Bauserman (2002) found that the positive effects of equal parenting for children are independent of parental conflict levels, as did Fabricius and Luecken (2007), who concluded that equal parenting responsibility is just as salutary for children in high conflict situations as for those in co-operative parenting arrangements. Fabricius, Diaz and Braver (2012) further determined that children's ongoing relationships with each parent can counter the harmful effects of parental conflict, and that limiting parental time when there is parental conflict makes children doubly vulnerable to long-term physical and mental health problems. Finally, as mentioned, Bauserman's (2012) meta-analysis of fifty North American studies examining parental conflict and adjustment in legal/physical joint custody and sole custody/primary residence families found that legal/physical joint custody and shared parenting was associated with significantly better outcomes than primary residence and sole custody in regard to parental conflict and re-litigation, and parental adjustment in general.

Adversarial legal processes that result in win-lose outcomes such as sole custody or primary residence seem tailor-made to produce or exacerbate high parental conflict, and it is no surprise that parental conflict levels are highest during the legal divorce transition. There is ample research that demonstrates this effect, as detailed in chapter 6. For example, Hawthorne and Lennings (2008) found that legal maternal custody and primary residence judgments, and the removal of fathers from children's daily routines, were correlated with fathers' increased anger and hostility toward their ex-wives. As discussed, parental conflict increases after sole custody and primary residence determinations and decreases with the establishment of equal or shared parenting arrangements, just as parental co-operation decreases with primary residence judgments, and increases in equal and shared parenting arrangements (Bauserman 2012 and 2002; Melli and Brown 2008). It is noteworthy that half of first-time family violence occurs after divorce, within the context of the sole custody/primary residence system (Ellis and Wight-Peasley 1986; Hotton 2003; Johnson and Hotton 2003; Statistics Canada 2008; Johnston, Roseby, and Kuehnle (2009) discuss the high prevalence of "separation-related violence" within adversarial child custody proceedings. This is no surprise given the high stakes involved; when primary parent-child relationships are threatened, the risk of violence rises dramatically. When neither parent is threatened by the loss of his or her children, conflict diminishes. The culture of animosity created by the sole custody system seems tailor-made to produce the worst possible outcomes when there are two capable parents who wish to continue as primary care-givers, cannot agree on a parenting plan, and are forced to dispar-age each other within the adversarial system in an effort to simply maintain their role as parents.

Within a sole custody or primary residence regime, conflict over access is often never-ending, as non-resident parents keep returning to court in an effort to gain more time with their chil-dren, with their efforts resisted by custodial parents who seek to lessen non-custodial parents' time in an effort to establish an orderly and uncomplicated living schedule, free from the interfer-ence of the non-residential parent. Sole custody is also an instiga-tion to escalate conflict, as "high conflict" becomes a weapon in some parents' attempts to prevail in child custody proceedings. The problem of perverse incentives to limit another parent's involvement (by exaggerating the amount of conflict that occurred, manufacturing allegations of abuse (the "hostile parent veto"), or instigating conflict to obtain a sole custody or primary residence order), has been discussed by a number of commenta-tors. Birnbaum and Bala (2010, 408) write: "There is a presump-tion in case law against joint custody in high conflict cases ... As a result, parents who seek sole custody often characterize their cases as high conflict. The parent exaggerates the extent of con-flict, or purposely engages in conflict to resist an order for joint custody." And judicial errors compromise children's safety; chil-dren of divorce are at risk when a parent is removed from their lives as a primary caregiver without a comprehensive investiga-tion, assessment, and recommendation by a competent child pro-tection authority. The parent mounting the stronger legal case often emerges as the winner in a child custody dispute; judges must make difficult decisions in the context of allegations and counter-allegations of abuse, alienation, and parental unfitness, but rarely is there any sort of criminal or child welfare investiga-tion of the allegations. The result is that in many cases custody is removed from a fit and loving parent and children end up in the sole care of the more adversarial, abusive, and alienating parent. Judicial errors in these cases lead to tragic outcomes (Richardson

2006); the potential for child abuse is virtually unchecked when complete authority over children is granted to parents in sole custody situations.

Equal- and shared-parental-responsibility arrangements do not increase inter-parental conflict (Bauserman 2002; Gunnoe and Braver 2001). Indeed, when neither parent is threatened by the loss of his or her children, conflict levels go down. Rather than accepting that high conflict is inevitable, the goal should be to reduce parental conflict after divorce. Most acrimonious parents can successfully learn to minimize conflict when motivated to do so, and an equal-parental-responsibility presumption provides an incentive for parental co-operation, negotiation, mediation, and the development of parenting plans (Kruk 2008). A number of specialized interventions to help parents reduce conflict have been developed, including therapeutic family mediation, parent education programs, parenting coordination, and parallel parenting. Parenting plans in particular make equal and shared parenting possible in high-conflict situations, as they provide a structure that limits parents' need for contact and communication. Key interventions in such cases include enhancing parents' attunement to children's needs (Moloney 2009), and a strengths-based approach. What we expect of others, they endeavour to provide: if we expect divorcing parents to be responsible and act in their children's best interests, and provide the supports to enable them to do so, they will act accordingly; if we expect them to fail, they will fail.

In sum, much of the "practice wisdom" regarding high conflict and equal parenting is not empirically supported, including the following assumptions: conflict is inherently bad for children; conflict will increase with equal parenting; equal parenting will not benefit children in high conflict situations; and little or nothing can be done to decrease conflict. Current literature challenges the position that equal and shared parenting is contraindicated in situations of high parental conflict, and the presence of parental conflict should not limit the possibility of children maintaining meaningful relationships with both of their parents (Lamb and Kelly 2009; Fabricius et al 2012; Fabricius and Luecken 2007). Similarly Nielsen (2013), in her review of the most recent research on shared residential custody, concludes that conflict should not be a factor in the legal determination of parenting after divorce, unless the conflict involves a documented history of physical abuse or violence.

4 *Equal parenting reflects children's preferences and views about their needs and best interests.*   Relatively few researchers have directly and systematically examined the perspective of children of divorce in regard to their needs and preferences regarding post-divorce living arrangements; those who have conclude that children strongly favour equal parenting (Fabricius 2003; Finley and Schwartz 2007). As discussed in chapter 5, recent studies have found that children of divorce consider equal time with their parents as the optimal living arrangement, and consider equal and shared parenting to be in their own and other children's best interests. In his large-scale (n=829) study of young adult children who had lived through their parents' divorces before the age of sixteen, Fabricius (2003) discovered that 70% of children of divorce believe that equal amounts of time with each parent is the best living arrangement for children of divorce generally, including 93% of children who were themselves raised in shared and equal-time homes. The latter were found to have the best relations with each of their parents after divorce, and reported outcomes far superior to those in primary residence homes, as children in sole custody arrangements articulated feelings of insecurity in their relationship with the non-residential parent, perception of rejection by that parent, and anger toward both their parents for denying them the opportunity for meaningful relationships with both parents. Consistent with this finding, Amato and Gilbreth (1999), in their earlier meta-analysis of studies of the post-divorce father-child post-divorce relationship, found that children who were more distant from their fathers had more problematic behavioural and emotional adjustment and lower school achievement. Derevensky and Deschamps (1997) and Lund (1987) reported similar results.

When children are asked directly about their own desired living arrangements and their opinions about what works best for children of divorce in general, they consistently report a strong preference for equal parenting, which they see as meeting their need for the meaningful involvement of both their parents in their lives, which they report as of paramount importance to their well-being. Although some studies suggest that the establishment and maintenance of equal and shared parenting pose challenges for children and express caution about the legal endorsement of such arrangements (Whitehead 2012), these are typically based on small, non-representative samples and do not provide respondents with the opportunity to express their actual preferences in regard to post-divorce living arrangements.

5 *Equal parenting reflects parents' preferences and views about their children's needs and best interests.* According to the majority of parents, the optimal post-divorce living arrangement, even in cases of high conflict, is equal parenting. Public opinion polls report that equal parental responsibility is favoured by about 80% of parents, with a slightly higher percentage of women favouring a legal presumption than men (Nanos Research 2009; Fabricius et al 2010). In a US study of 267 people who had been summoned for jury duty, 70% believed that children of divorce should live in equal-time arrangements with each parent, although only 28% believed that a judge would make such a decision (Braver et al 2011). On the matter of parenting after divorce, there thus is a marked disconnection between public opinion and the opinion of legal professionals (Pruett, Hoganbruen, and Jackson 2000), with changing public opinion reflecting an ongoing cultural evolution of parenting values and norms. Divorce law and policy must reflect contemporary cultural standards, and both the judiciary and legislatures would be ill-advised to ignore the strong public support for equal parental responsibility and the equally strong public condemnation of the courts as unreasonably gender-biased in regard to parenting after divorce (Fabricius et al 2010). The law walks a dangerous line when it deviates substantially from an emerging community consensus such as equal parenting (Maldonado 2005); at the same time, the success of an equal-parental-responsibility

presumption is enhanced by the coincidence of this law reform effort and community opinion.

Kruk's (2010a, 2010b) research on divorced fathers' and mothers' perspectives on their children's needs, and parental and social institutional responsibilities in relation to those needs, found that parents define their children's best interests as commensurate with the active involvement of both parents in children's lives in a shared care arrangement. Seventy-eight percent of divorced fathers and 86% of non-custodial mothers in these studies identified equal parental responsibility as the legal presumption most in keeping with their children's best interests.

6 *Equal parenting reflects child caregiving arrangements before divorce.* It is now well established that children form primary attachment bonds with each of their parents (Rutter 1995; Lamb and Kelly 2009). Further, with the "gender convergence" of child care roles, shared parental responsibility has emerged as the norm in two-parent families (Atwood 2007; Marshall 2006; Bianchi, Robinson, and Milkie 2006). As detailed in chapter 5, North American time budget analyses report that fathers have significantly increased their participation in family work tasks over the past two decades. This is particularly evident in regard to child care, according to Health Canada's National Work-Life Conflict Study (Higgins and Duxbury 2002 and 2012): on average, mothers who work outside the home spend an average of 11.1 hours on direct child care tasks per week; fathers devote 10.5 hours, a 51–49% split of child care tasks (Higgins and Duxbury 2002 and 2012). Another study found that although working longer hours outside the home than mothers, young fathers spend an average of 4.3 hours a day with their children, only 45 minutes less than mothers (Galinsky, Aumann, and Bond 2009). An equal-parental-responsibility presumption thus most closely reflects child caregiving arrangements before divorce; claims that mothers are the primary caregivers of children before divorce (Boyd 2003) are outdated and no longer supported by empirical evidence.

7 *Equal parenting enhances the quality of parent-child relationships.* An equal-parental-responsibility presumption provides a context and climate for the continuation or development of high quality parent-child relationships, allowing parents to remain authoritative, responsible, involved, attached, emotionally available, supportive, and focused on children's day-to-day lives (Flouri 2005). Attachment bonds are formed through mutual participation in daily routines, including bedtime and waking rituals, transitions to and from school, and extracurricular and recreational activities (Lamb and Kelly 2009; Fabricius et al 2010), and parents need ample time with their children in order to create and maintain relationships of quality (Amato and Dorius 2012). Quantity is necessary for quality, and there is a direct correlation between quantity of time and quality of parent-child relationships, as high quality relationships between parents and children are not possible without sufficient, routine time to develop and sustain such quality relationships (Amato and Dorius 2012; Lamb and Kelly 2009; Kruk 2010a; Fabricius et al 2010; Fabricius et al 2011). For children, attachment and feelings of "mattering," feeling prioritized, cared for, and cared about, emotionally as well as physically (Trinder 2009), are not possible within the constraints of visitation. For parents, quality of relationships with children are compromised both in cases in which a parent is overwhelmed by sole custodial responsibility and in cases in which a parent feels disenfranchised as a non-resident parent. The constraints of traditional "access" relationships are well documented (Kelly 2007; Kruk 1993b); closeness, warmth, and mutual understanding are elusive when parenting within the constraints of thin slices of time (Smyth 2009). Meaningful relationships are developed and sustained through emotional connectedness (Moloney 2009), made possible through the emotional stability and security of equal parenting time. At the same time, quality of parent-child relationships is enhanced when parents do not feel burdened or overwhelmed by the demands of sole parental responsibility; studies have consistently reported that joint custody parents report significantly less burden and stress in their lives than sole custody/primary

residence parents, as sole responsibility for day-to-day attention to the child's needs is not placed on either the mother or the father, resulting in better quality parent-child relationships (Bauserman 2012).

Finally, it comes as no surprise, as recent studies have reported (Bauserman 2012), that the highest and lowest levels of parental satisfaction with parenting arrangements after divorce are found in sole custody/primary residence families: custodial or primary residential parents report the highest levels of satisfaction with parenting after divorce arrangements, whereas non-custodial/non-residential parents the lowest. Between these extremes lies equal parenting, as joint legal/physical custody is associated with similar levels of satisfaction between mothers and fathers (Kaspiew et al 2009). The imbalance in parental satisfaction levels between primary residential and non-residential parenting arrangements does not bode well for the exercise of parental rights and responsibilities after divorce, as one parent remains at a significant disadvantage in regard to quality of life and well-being. Parental quality of life is an important and significant determinant of the quality of parent-child relationships.

8 Equal parenting decreases parental focus on "mathematizing time" and reduces litigation.   According to Smyth (2009), too much of the debate about parenting after divorce remains stuck in "mathematizing time." An equal-parental-responsibility presumption, defined both in terms of the approximation standard and as equal time division, frees parents and the judiciary from ongoing disputes over amounts of contact time to be spent by the non-resident parent with the children. When one parent is the primary custodial parent, ongoing litigation over access time for the non-custodial parent is prevalent.

Conflict is fuelled by the adversarial nature of contested child custody; an equal-parental-responsibility presumption reduces strategic bargaining, hostile negotiations, and litigation, and removes parenting after divorce from the adversarial arena. The intensified anger and hostility attendant to litigation has a deep emotional impact on children in particular (Pruett and Jackson

1999). In addition, the scarcity of resources and financial insecurity resulting from ongoing litigation accounts for much of the negative impact of divorce for all family members (Semple 2010). Less hostile dispute resolution processes are a key factor contributing to quality co-parenting relationships (Bonach 2005).

An equal-parental-responsibility presumption also addresses the problem of one-shoe-fits-all arrangements prevalent in sole custody determinations, such as limiting access to every second weekend for the non-resident parent. An equal parental responsibility approach guides parents toward the development of individualized parenting plans, resulting in greater variety of outcomes. Children of different ages and stages of development require different schedules, and an equal-parental-responsibility presumption leads to parenting arrangements tailor-made to needs of each individual child and family – an infinite variety of shared parenting arrangements are possible. The equal parental responsibility model proposed in chapter 8 applies the approximation standard in cases of dispute, apportioning 50–50 time when both parents are primary caregivers, scheduled according to children's ages and stages of development.

9 *Equal parenting provides an incentive for inter-parental negotiation, mediation, and the development of co-operative parenting plans.* As Emery (2007) argues, parental self-determination should be the overriding goal of legal custody determinations. Within a best-interests-of-the-child / sole custody system, however, there is little incentive for parents who foresee winning sole custody, or who are determined to punish their former spouses, to engage in a process of assisted negotiation. An equal-parental-responsibility presumption would provide such an incentive, with processes such as mediation focused on the development of a parenting plan.

An equal-parental-responsibility presumption will not work without adequate supports in place, such as family relationship centres, therapeutic family mediation, parent education programs, and parenting coordination, especially in high conflict situations. At the same time, an equal-parental-responsibility presumption not only encourages the uptake of such support services by parents, but also puts pressure on legislatures to develop programs that will enable parents to negotiate parenting plans. The experience of jurisdictions that have moved toward establishing an equal-parental-responsibility presumption makes this clear; increased use of family relationship centres and family mediation services in Australia has resulted in 72% of parents now being able to resolve post-divorce parenting arrangements without the use of legal services (Kaspiew et al 2010; Kaspiew et al 2009).

An equal-parental-responsibility presumption also allows the option of parallel parenting in situations of high conflict between parents, which protects children from parental conflict while protecting their relationships with both parents, as parents continue parenting in a disengaged manner; over time, as the dust settles and parents begin to separate their former marital hostilities from their ongoing parental responsibilities, parallel arrangements gradually give way to co-operative parenting (Birnbaum and Fidler 2005).

10 *Equal parenting provides a clear and consistent guideline for judicial decision-making.* As discussed in chapter 4, the best-interests-of-the-child standard is indeterminate and promotes litigation, a highly destructive process for all family members. Criteria respecting the best interests of the child are rarely defined in legislation; the nebulous nature of these criteria, and their vulnerability to value preferences, has resulted in a situation in which judges are guided by any number of idiosyncratic biases regarding children's best interests. Child development and family dynamics are a delicate matter, and the discretionary power of judges an area in which they are neither professionally trained, nor competent to assess third-party evaluations or professional literature on the matter, is a recipe for disaster. In making decisions regarding parenting after divorce, child custody, and access, judges do not consult relevant research on child outcomes (Kelly and Lamb 2000), and are highly susceptible to error bias (Firestone and Weinstein 2004; McMurray and Blackmore 1992): judges are not infallible and routinely make mistakes, awarding

custody to the more litigious parent, with children running the risk of being placed in the exclusive care of an abusive parent. Melton (1989) presents a startling account of how little social science knowledge trickles down into legal policies that are intended to benefit children in the parenting after divorce realm. In the case of two fit and loving parents, the act of judges privileging one parent over the other as a residential parent, thereby removing one from the child's life as a custodial parent, thus lacks foundation. And although judges determine custody in a relatively small proportion of cases, these decisions have profound repercussions for the larger proportion of non-adjudicated cases, as fathers in particular do not contest custody when they believe their chances of success are small (Kruk 1991).

A legal presumption such as equal parental responsibility in contested parenting after divorce, a clear-cut default rule, removes speculation about future conduct as a basis for making custody decisions, limits judicial discretion, enhances determinacy and predictability of outcome, and reduces litigation and hostility. It eliminates the need for courts to adjudicate between two fit and loving parents, or to remove one parent as a primary caregiver. It also provides an anchor for negotiation for those who bargain in the shadow of the law. As Emery (2007) points out, a legal presumption does not abandon children's best interests, but provides a clear, evidence-based definition of children's needs in the divorce transition.

In sum, an equal-parental-responsibility presumption eliminates unnecessary complexity, and simplifies that which has increasingly been made unnecessarily complex in parenting after divorce disputes. As Burgoyne, Ormrod, and Richards (1987) asked many years ago about parenting after divorce, "Why courts at all?" Within marriage, custody is held jointly and equally by both parents and it may be questioned whether the courts should even be involved in changing that situation. Indeed, this could be put more positively: at the end of a marriage or common-law union the law would simply reaffirm the role of both parents and make clear that although the divorce is the end of the parents' relationship, their parental rights and responsibilities continue. An equal-parental-responsibility presumption allows the court to make no order at all about custody so that the situation that existed in the marriage could simply continue, thereby removing the court system from unnecessary intrusion in family life when there are two "good enough" parents in disagreement over parenting after divorce. An equal-parental-responsibility presumption would allow the court to disengage from those cases in which a child is not in need of protection.

11 *Equal parenting reduces the risk and incidence of parental alienation.* For children, parental alienation is trauma writ large, as they lose the joy and love of their previous relationship with a parent, and this affects a sizeable number of children of divorce (Bernet et al 2010; Baker 2005; Bala, Hunt, and McCarney 2010). There is consensus among researchers that severe alienation is abusive to children (Fidler and Bala 2010); the removal of a fit and loving parent as a primary caregiver from the life of a child, some have argued, is in itself a form of parental alienation, as children are robbed of their parent's routine care and nurture, as well as that of their extended family.

Parental alienation flourishes in situations in which one parent has exclusive care and control of children, as sole residential custody is at times granted to parents with serious psychological problems who mount the stronger case in the adversarial arena (McMurray and Blackmore 1992). An equal-parental-responsibility presumption reduces the risk and incidence of parental alienation, and the forced disengagement and absence of non-custodial parents, because children continue to maintain meaningful routine relationships with both of their parents, and are thus less susceptible to the toxic influence of an alienating parent. At the same time, with equal parental responsibility neither parent is threatened by the potential loss of their relationship with their children, and each is less likely to denigrate the other parent in an effort to bolster their own sense of parental identity and obtain a primary residence order.

12 *Equal parenting enables enforcement of parenting orders, as parents are more likely to abide by an equal-parental-responsibility order.* Primary residence orders with periodic access provisions

for non-resident parents have presented a law enforcement nightmare, with non-custodial parents vying for more time with children while custodial parents attempt to limit that parent's involvement. Access denial is endemic in sole custody families (Kruk 2010a); in the case of non-residential parents, refusal to comply with sole custody orders is more likely because they are perceived as inherently unfair or unequal. Rank-ordering of parents fuels discord (Warshak 2007), but with equal parental responsibility, neither parent's relationship with their children nor their parental identity is threatened, and neither parent is constrained by the limitations of a "visiting" relationship (Kelly 2007; Kruk 1993b). This makes enforcement less of a problem, as parents are more likely to abide by an equal parental responsibility order they perceive as fair, than a sole custody "winner-loser" determination that they believe either gives them veto power over visits or is inherently biased (Brinig 2001).

13 *Equal parenting addresses social justice imperatives regarding protection of children's rights.* An equal-parental-responsibility presumption ensures equal legal protection of parent-child relationships for children of divorce, under the anti-discrimination provisions of the UN Convention on the Rights of the Child. Whereas sole custody practice and legislation permitting removal of parental custody subsequent to divorce discriminates against children of divorce (permitting judges to remove custody from a parent and a parent from children's lives on the basis of the indeterminate, discretionary best-interests-of-the-child standard, as opposed to the more stringent child-in-need-of-protection standard for all other children), equal parental responsibility ensures equal protection of parent-child relationships for all children, regardless of parental marital status. This double standard violates Article 2 of the UN Convention, as it applies a different standard to children whose parents divorce, to warrant parental removal, to that applied to children in two-parent families. An equal-parental-responsibility presumption applies the more stringent child-in-need-of-protection standard to warrant parental removal, which necessitates thorough investigation by a

competent child welfare authority, the standard applied with children in two-parent families. An equal-parental-responsibility presumption establishes a child's right to be raised by both parents and to preserve primary relationships with each of them.

14 *Equal parenting addresses social justice imperatives regarding parental authority, autonomy, equality, rights, and responsibilities.* Rights and responsibilities are correlative, as parental rights are needed to enable parents to successfully carry out their parental responsibilities, and parental authority in children's lives is an effect of parentage. An equal-parental-responsibility presumption avoids having the rights of one parent being opposed to those of the other, and avoids privileging the rights of one parent over the other. An equal-parental-responsibility presumption affirms the equality of parents as primary caregivers, and as equally capable and salient in the lives of their children. As Kelly and Johnston (2005) point out, there is no basis in law or psychology for preferring one parent to the other, or for choosing between two "good enough" parents contesting custody.

Unequal parenting arrangements are perceived by parents as inherently unfair, and these are more likely to break down subsequent to divorce than equal parental responsibility arrangements (Warshak 2007; Melli and Brown 2008; Brinig 2001). This includes "unequal" shared parenting arrangements such as 70–30 or 60–40 divisions of child care responsibility, which are associated with higher levels of parental discord than equal 50–50 time share arrangements (Melli and Brown 2008; Kaspiew et al 2009). Contrary to earlier reports that joint custody arrangements gradually revert to maternal custody with the passage of time, although the level of involvement of both parents remains high in children's lives (Juby, Marcil-Gratton, and LeBourdais 2004), recent research has shown that shared and equal parenting are stable over time (Berger et al 2008; Cashmore and Parkinson 2010), especially in situations in which they reflect pre-divorce caregiving patterns (Brinig 2001). Melli and Brown (2008) found that three years after divorce, 90% of children initially in shared care arrangements were still living in dual residences. The perception among parents is that equal time is fair and allows for equality of opportunity between the parents in their rights and responsibilities toward their children.

15 The discretionary best-interests-of-the-child/sole custody model is not empirically supported. The evidence of the failure and harms of the sole custody/primary residence model vis-à-vis children, parents, and extended family members is abundant. Primary residence orders are associated both with diminished parent-child relationships, leading in some cases to the absence of a parent from children's lives, and with exacerbation of conflict between parents, and leading in some cases to incidents of first-time family violence. The effects of these phenomena are particularly damaging to children: disrupted parent-child relationships contribute to emotional insecurity in children, and compromised mental and emotional well-being, and heightened conflict between parents compromises children's physical security and well-being. Yet, as Kelly (1991) writes, the pattern of awarding primary residence to one parent with intermittent "visitation" granted to the other continues, not subject to the degree of scrutiny and challenge it deserves. But legislatures continue to enact or maintain laws and family judges issue residential orders that directly contradict empirical research data and the teachings of child psychologists and sociologists specializing in child welfare.

16 A rebuttable legal presumption of equal parenting responsibility is empirically supported. The empirical evidence of the effectiveness of equal parenting as a viable alternative to a sole custody approach is robust, as there are now over two dozen studies comparing child outcomes in primary residence versus equal and shared parenting arrangements that demonstrate that children adjust significantly better in equal and shared parenting arrangements, even in high conflict situations. Bauserman's 2002 and 2012 meta-analyses compared child and parent outcomes in sole and joint custody settings and found significantly better outcomes for children in joint custody homes on all measures of general and divorce-specific adjustment. Although many of the studies reviewed by Bauserman compared self-selected joint custody families with sole custody families, several included legally mandated joint-physical-custodial arrangements, in which joint custody was ordered over the objections of the parents. These families fared as well as the self-selected samples, confirming the findings of earlier studies that joint custody works equally well for conflictual families in which parents are vying for custody (Benjamin and Irving 1989; Brotsky, Steinman, and Zemmelman 1988). Bauserman also found that inter-parental co-operation increases over time in shared custody arrangements, and decreases in sole custody arrangements.

The research evidence for equal parental responsibility is strong; studies by Braver and O'Connell (1998), Gunnoe and Braver (2002), Fabricius (2003), Fabricius and Luecken (2007), Fabricius et al (2010), Fabricius et al (2011), Kelly (2007), Kelly and Johnston (2005), Warshak (2003a), Bauserman (2002), Finley and Schwartz (2007), Lamb and Kelly (2009), Lamb (2004), Campana et al (2008), and Millar (2009) among others report salutary outcomes for children of divorce in equal parental responsibility arrangements. These studies have found that parent-child relationship security attendant within an equal parental responsibility arrangement is strongly associated with child well-being, and that children in equal parenting arrangements score lowest on both depression and aggression, even in high conflict situations. The mounting evidence in support of equal parental responsibility reflects an emerging consensus on the issue of parenting after divorce, with equal- and shared-parental-responsibility arrangements considered to be optimal for the great majority of children of divorce whose parents are in dispute (Fabricius et al 2010; Bauserman 2012; Nielsen 2013).

As equal parental responsibility is an emergent pattern of care, and not implemented in pure form in any jurisdiction, research evidence from jurisdictions with an equal-parental-responsibility presumption is somewhat tentative. Most studies have utilized small and unrepresentative samples, or data sets in which only custodial or residential parents' views were sought. Nevertheless, the Australian Institute of Family Studies' (Kaspiew et al 2009) review of equal parental responsibility legislation indicates that an equal-parental-responsibility presumption is widely supported by both parents and professionals, and is beneficial and working well for children, including children under the age of three, according to parents; child custody litigation rates have dropped, and there is a corresponding increase in the use of mediation and family dispute resolution services; most parents are able to resolve their conflict within a year after divorce without the use of legal services, and are making use of family relationship services; equal parental responsibility arrangements are durable; and there is no evidence that high conflict has a more negative effect for children in equal parental responsibility arrangements than for those in sole custody homes. What remains an issue of concern in Australia is the lack of application of a presumption against equal parental responsibility in family violence situations, a cornerstone of the equal parental responsibility approach proposed in the following chapter.

8

The Equal-Parental-Responsibility Presumption: A Four-Pillar Approach to the Legal Determination of Parenting after Divorce

THE LEGAL PRESUMPTION OF EQUAL PARENTAL RESPONSIBILITY

It is generally agreed among divorce scholars, practitioners, and policymakers that any reform of parenting after divorce law must ensure that children's basic needs and interests are addressed to the fullest extent possible. This requires an understanding of children's fundamental needs in the divorce transition and a corresponding set of parental and societal responsibilities to those needs. As the preceding chapters have shown, a new, non-discretionary standard of the best interests of the child from the perspective of the child is required, which includes serious consideration of what children themselves have identified as their core needs in the divorce transition; they are most affected by parental divorce and thus are the real "experts" on the matter. By their own account, three essential elements stand out for children of divorce, as identified by Fabricius (2003) and others: autonomy and the opportunity to identify their own best interests in the divorce transition; protection from conflict and violence between their parents; and substantially equal time in their relationships with each of their parents.

From listening to the voices of children of divorce, we now have clear evidence of a fundamentally different perceptive of divorce and parenting after divorce than what most policymakers and legislators have assumed. Most children want to be in the shared physical care of their parents after divorce (Fabricius 2003; Fabricius and Hall 2000), and research studies support their stated preferences: children in equal or shared parenting arrangements adjust significantly better than those in sole custody arrangements on all general and divorce-specific adjustment measures. At the same time, the research has demonstrated that the reduction of parental conflict and increased parental cooperation after divorce, critical to children's well-being, are most likely to be attained via equal and shared parenting. Two key factors are associated with children's best interests, and are thus fundamental to divorce and parenting-after-divorce law reform: the necessity of preserving children's primary relationships with both parents, beyond the constraints of traditional "visiting" and "access" relationships; and the fundamental need to address the problems of family violence and ongoing high conflict between parents in the divorce transition. Any new framework for the legal determination of parenting after divorce should be examined carefully in regard to the degree to which parent-child relationships are preserved and conflict and violence are reduced between parents.

Despite an emergent consensus on children's needs in divorce, the current parenting after divorce policy debate in Canada has been framed in a way that has overlooked some key questions, especially in light of what children and parents define as the most important considerations, and what research has revealed about child and family functioning after divorce. Why are parents with no civil or criminal wrongdoing forced to surrender their rights and responsibilities to raise their children? Why do courts discriminate against children and families of divorce by applying the indeterminate best-interests-of-the-child standard to remove parents from children's lives, as opposed to the more determinate child-in-need-of-protection standard for non-divorced parents? On what basis do courts justify treating parents unequally, as "custodial" and "non-custodial" or "residential" and "non-residential" parents? Why are children forced to surrender their need for both parents? Why are social institutions such as the courts undermining, rather than supporting, parents in the fulfillment of their parental responsibilities? Is the removal of a fit and loving parent from the life of a child, in the absence of an investigated child protection finding, a form of systemic abuse, if indeed children need both their mothers and fathers as active parents in their lives following parental divorce, and to be protected from ongoing high conflict and violence between their parents?

In Canada, when divorces occur and parents cannot agree on child caregiving arrangements, courts become involved in custody determination and one parent's role typically becomes extremely marginalized. Because of the bias and prejudices inherent in the discretionary best-interests-of-the-child standard, resulting in judicial determinations of sole custody or primary residence in the great majority of litigated cases, children's need for a paternal influence in particular has been largely ignored (Millar 2009; Baskerville 2007). Yet fathers are no less primary than mothers in their children's lives, and an access-based "visiting" relationship in no way resembles active parenting, which requires routine involvement in the daily tasks of caregiving (Kruk 1993b; Arditti and Prouty 1999; Kelly 2000; Kelly and Lamb 2000).

Further, the sole custody/primary residence system, in which the more aggressive and privileged party in a custody litigation holds a distinct advantage, exacerbates conflict. The language used in custody law has created and maintained expectations about ownership and rights, and who "wins" and "loses." Most important, the winner-take-all approach, in heightening conflict between former spouses, often leads to tragic outcomes. It is critical that post-divorce living arrangements reduce conflict between parents, and that support services are available at the time of divorce to shield children from destructive parental conflict.

The guidelines for parenting-after-divorce law reform proposed by the Special Joint Committee on Child Custody and Access, the Federal/Provincial/Territorial Family Law Committee, and the Child-Centred Family Justice Strategy, discussed in chapter 3, acknowledge that any effective law reform effort will have to incorporate these elements as the foundation for a just and equitable approach to parenting after divorce in conflicted cases. Above all else, these reports reflect a child-focused approach that emphasizes children's needs and parental responsibilities over custodial rights, and attends to children's well-being and best interests in the divorce transition. Such an approach is the cornerstone of current divorce and parenting-after-divorce law reform initiatives in Europe, the United States, and Australia. A responsibility-to-needs framework, which focuses on children's needs, parental responsibilities to those needs, and the responsibilities of social institutions to support parents in the fulfillment of their parental responsibilities, is gradually supplanting a rights-based approach to parenting after divorce (Kruk 2008).

At the same time, a new approach to parenting after divorce must also attend to the needs of mothers and fathers; although children's needs are distinct from those of their parents, they are inextricably linked. New legislation must take on board the concerns of both feminist and fathers' advocacy groups, including feminist concerns regarding family violence, the recognition of primary caregiving, and problems with awarding legal joint custody without any corresponding responsibility for child care involvement, as well as fathers' concerns about their disenfranchisement from children's lives, the importance of preserving emotional attachments between children and both parents, parental alienation, and enforcement of parenting orders.

Finally, divorce and parenting-after-divorce law reform needs to go beyond cosmetic changes such as changing the language of divorce, and also beyond equal or shared parenting legislation that retains the discretionary best-interests-of-the-child standard. A new approach will need to ensure determinacy and consistency in decision-making, and remove discretion in areas in which judges have no expertise. The challenge is to develop and establish a legal presumption that minimizes judicial discretion, enhances determinacy and reduces litigation, while at the same time serving the best interests of the child and taking into account each child and family's unique circumstances.

A best-interests-of-the-child-from-the-perspective-of-the-child standard and responsibility-to-needs approach to parenting after divorce must in the first instance remove the indeterminate best-interests-of-the-child criterion and define precisely what constitutes children's best interests in divorce, enumerating these core needs and interests. In the empirical research on the needs and well-being of children of divorce, researchers identify the following key factors as constituting children's core needs in the divorce transition:

1 *Parents' desires and specific plans for post-divorce parenting* As parents are most knowledgeable about their children's needs and interests, in cases in which parents are in dispute over post-divorce parenting arrangements, it is important to children's well-being to establish the nature of parents' desires regarding and future commitment to raising their children: their specific parenting plans. This would include the degree to which each parent is willing to make accommodations for the needs of the children, and the extent to which each is able to adjust his or her employment and living arrangements to allow sufficient time and energy for their parenting responsibilities.

2 *Parents' relationship history with their children* The time and effort each parent has invested in child caregiving is a second key element in regard to children's needs and interests. How involved and available, empathic, and attuned is each parent to his or her children's needs? In the interests of stability and continuity in children's lives, a parenting arrangement that approximates existing parent-child relationships as much as possible is important to children's well-being.

3 *Children's need for both parents actively involved in their lives* Research is clear that an equal parenting arrangement best assures the continued meaningful involvement of both parents in children's lives, a vital component of children's well-being after divorce.

4 *Children's need to be shielded from family violence and child abuse* It is vitally important that allegations and reports of family violence and abuse be fully and expeditiously investigated, and that children be protected from violence and abuse.

The equal parenting presumption outlined below fully incorporates each of these elements, and is unique on several planes. First, it is a child-focused framework that takes on board not only empirical research findings on the needs and best interests of children of divorce, but also the primary concerns of both feminist and father advocacy groups. Second, the framework merges a rebuttable legal presumption of equal parenting responsibility with a rebuttable presumption against equal parental responsibility in cases of established family violence and child abuse. Third, it confronts the problem of discrimination against children of divorce on the basis of parental status, as it adopts a child-in-need-of-protection criterion rather than the discretionary best-interests-of-the-child standard to determine the need for the removal of a parental from children's lives. Fourth, it is a hybrid of the "approximation standard" and suggests an equal 50–50 parenting time apportionment (equal parenting or joint physical custody), but also incorporates elements of a "parenting plan" approach and primary caregiver presumption. The equal parental presumption outlined below transcends the subjectivity of the discretionary best-interests-of-the-child standard while at the same time taking into account children's and families' individual and unique circumstances. In sum, the four pillars detailed below operationalize both a best-interests-of-the-child-from-the-perspective-of-the-child legal criterion and a responsibility-to-needs approach to parenting after divorce.

THE FOUR PILLARS OF LEGAL DETERMINATION OF PARENTING AFTER DIVORCE

In essence, the stated objectives of proposed Canadian legislative reform to parenting after divorce are to promote ongoing, meaningful relationships between children and both of their parents following separation and divorce, to encourage parental co-operation, and to reduce parental conflict and litigation. Further, legislative reform should encourage parents to restructure their relationships in a way that promotes the best interests of children; that is, to focus their attention on the needs and well-being of their children during the divorce transition.

Although a one-size-fits-all model of the legal determination of parenting after divorce is ill-advised, clarity and predictability of outcome are important, as unfettered judicial discretion regarding determination of the best interests of the child has failed to ensure the health and well-being of children and families. In light of the diversity of parenting structures and patterns in Canada, a one-size-fits-all approach, whether it is sole custody or equal parenting, will not meet the needs of all children and families. The law must allow for flexibility to address the different circumstances of children and families. At the same time, legislation must provide clear guidelines for custody determination.

The salience of preserving primary parent-child attachments and relationships, on the one hand, to children's well-being, on the other, cannot be overstated. More than any other factor, the maintenance of meaningful relationships with both parents is vital to children of divorce. At the same time, reform must ensure that children are protected from family violence and abuse. Cases of established child abuse, which include children witnessing the abuse of a parent, it is generally agreed, require a court determination of custody as well as criminal proceedings. Cases in which family violence and child abuse are not legally established, and there is no finding that a child is in need of protection from a parent, lend themselves to an equal or shared parenting arrangement, involving either co-operative or parallel parenting (Jaffe, Crooks, and Bala 2005), as children are best supported when parents assume shared responsibility and when social institutions such as the courts support parents in the fulfillment of their parental obligations.

The following four-pillar framework is a viable socio-legal policy solution to the problems resulting from adversarially based custody determination:

1 Legal Presumption of Equal Parental Responsibility: Best-interests-of-the-child-from-the-perspective-of-the-child standard and responsibility-to-needs approach

2 Treatment: Divorce education, mediation, and support/intervention in high-conflict cases

3 Prevention: Equal parenting public education

4 Enforcement: Judicial determination in cases of established abuse and enforcement of equal parental responsibility orders

Pillar 1: Legal Presumption of Equal Parental Responsibility

The first pillar of the model is intended to operationalize the best-interests-of-the-child-from-the-perspective-of-the-child standard and responsibility-to-needs principle by means of a legal presumption of equal parental responsibility, a rebuttable presumption of joint physical custody in family law. A rebuttable presumption of equal parenting responsibility in contested parenting-after-divorce cases would be defined as children spending equal amounts of time in each parent's household. This pillar is itself comprised of four stages:

1 Parenting Plan Requirement (applied to all parents in dispute): a legal requirement that parents develop a parenting plan before any hearing is held on the matter of parenting after divorce;

2 Approximation Rule (applied to parents who cannot agree on a parenting plan): legal application of the "approximation rule" when parents cannot agree on a parenting plan with children spending time with each parent in proportion to the relative amount of time each parent devoted to child care before divorce;

3 Equal Parenting Time (applied to parents who were both primary caregivers before divorce): legal application of a rebuttable presumption of equal parenting time when both parents were or claim to have been primary caregivers of their children before divorce;

4 Presumption Against Equal Parenting Responsibility (applied when it is established that a child is in need of protection):

legal application of a rebuttable presumption against equal parenting in cases in which it is established that a child is in need of protection from a parent, with the court making a custody determination.

This four-stage process represents a highly individualized approach to the legal determination of parenting after divorce, taking into account the unique situation and circumstances of each individual child and family, detailed below.

1 *Parenting Plan Requirement: Establish a legal expectation that parents develop a parenting plan before any court hearing is held on the matter of parenting after divorce.*   The role of the court would be to legally sanction the parenting plan or agreement, whether sole, shared, or equal. Parents would have a choice of developing the plan jointly though direct negotiation, legal negotiation, or family mediation; court-based or independent family mediation and family support services would be focused on assisting parents in the development of the plan. Parents would not be required to negotiate face to face, but would be encouraged and supported to negotiate in the future, as any post-divorce parenting arrangement requires some degree of ongoing communication. This legal expectation would place an onus on parents in dispute to work out their own arrangements rather than to surrender decision-making to the court system; parents would be deemed to have the capacity to resolve their own disputes and would be acknowledged as the experts in regard to their children's best interests. They would develop a parenting plan tailored to their children's ages and stages of development, their own schedules, and their children's unique needs. Parental autonomy and self-determination in regard to post-divorce parenting arrangements would thus be the cornerstone of family law.

2 *Approximation Rule: Establish a legal expectation that in cases in which parents cannot agree on a parenting plan, existing parent-child relationships will continue after divorce.*   In cases of dispute regarding post-divorce parenting arrangements, the approximation rule will be the legal standard, so that the relative

proportion of time children spend with each parent after divorce will be equal to the relative proportion of time each parent spent performing child caregiving functions before divorce. As a form of equal parenting, the "approximation rule" (discussed in chapter 4), is individualized, child-focused, and gender neutral. It also provides judges with a clear guideline and avoids the dilemma of judges adjudicating children's best interests in the absence of expertise in this arena. Children's needs to maintain relationships with each parent, and to have stability and continuity in regard to their routines and living arrangements, would thus be addressed; and parents' needs for a fair, gender-neutral criterion would also be accommodated. The approximation standard, drafted by feminist scholar Katharine Bartlett for the American Law Institute, incorporates feminist concerns regarding parenting after divorce (Brinig 2001), but also addresses fathers' concerns regarding the maintenance of meaningful relationships with children after divorce. Given the gender convergence in regard to division of child care tasks and the emerging norm of shared parental responsibility for child care in two-parent families (Atwood 2007; Marshall 2006), the approximation criterion will translate to roughly equal time apportionment in most disputed cases of parenting after divorce.

3 *Equal Parenting Time: Establish a rebuttable legal presumption of equal parenting time in cases in which both parents were primary caregivers before divorce and are in dispute over the relative proportion of time each parent spent performing child caregiving functions before divorce.* A preoccupation with the amount of time spent with each parent is the Achilles' heel of the approximation standard, and tracking parental time devoted to children's care before divorce is a dauntingly complex task (Lamb 2007; Warshak 2007). Because some parents will dispute each other's estimates of past time devoted to child care, with "mathematizing time" a focus of conflict, in the interests of shielding children from ongoing conflict, an equal parenting time-division would be the legal norm in cases in which both parents were primary caregivers before divorce, or claim to have been

primary caregivers. Again, in addition to being child-focused and gender neutral, this presumption will provide judges with a clear guideline and will avoid the dilemma of judges adjudicating the relative amount of time each parent spent in caregiving tasks before divorce.

Both the approximation rule and equal time presumption are primarily intended to maximize the involvement of both parents in their children's lives after divorce. Equal parental responsibility results in a division of parenting time which allows each parent a meaningful level of involvement and responsibility for children, while at the same time providing each a respite from full-time child rearing, which is particularly important when, as is the case in most Canadian families, both parents work full-time. It is also intended to maximize parental co-operation and reduce conflict after parental divorce.

A legal presumption of equal parental responsibility establishes an expectation that the former partners are of equal status before the law in regard to their parental rights and responsibilities, and conveys to children the message that their parents are of equal value as parents. At the same time, in the interests of stability and continuity in children's relationships with their parents, pre-existing parent-child relationships would be expected to continue after divorce, at least in the initial divorce transition period. This would ensure that there is no sharp discontinuity of parent-child relationships, as exists at present in most sole custody awards. To the extent that "history of care" and "cultural, linguistic, religious, and spiritual upbringing and heritage" are cited as important vis-à-vis children's needs for roots and security in maintaining existing relationships, the idea of the immutability of parent-child relationships is important to convey to divorcing parents. The adjudicative role of the courts would be reduced with the legal expectation that post-divorce parenting arrangements reflect (in proportionate time) pre-divorce parenting patterns. The approximation standard would also provide an incentive for greater parental involvement in children's lives before divorce; because the rule looks to historical practices before divorce, it encourages parents to invest in pre-divorce parenting. Thus, the approximation rule would be practical for implementing a useful social norm (Atwood 2007). If the active involvement of both parents is critical to children's well-being after divorce, then it should also be beneficial to them before.

In cases in which parents dispute the relative amount of time each spent in child caregiving before divorce, the court would apply an equal-time/joint-physical-custody presumption and not get drawn into investigations regarding the proportionate amount of time each parent spent with the children prior to divorce. Although it is a blunt instrument, and "children spending equal time with each of their parents" after divorce may not reflect de facto the existing arrangements in the pre-divorce household, a rebuttable equal parenting presumption would divert parents from a destructive court battle over their children's care. Equal parental responsibility is also in keeping with current caregiving patterns, as the majority of mothers and fathers are now sharing responsibility for child care in two-parent families.

A presumption of equal parental responsibility is thus a much more individualized approach than the one-size-fits-all formula of sole custody, a blunt instrument which forcefully removes a parent from the life of a child in contested cases. First, parents are free to make whatever arrangements they wish on their own and, second, if they cannot decide, a presumption in which post-divorce parenting arrangements approximate as closely as possible the existing arrangements in the two-parent family would be applied, in the interest of stability for children. Third, it is only in cases in which both parents present as primary caregivers and cannot agree on a parenting plan that a presumption of equal time parenting would apply, in the interests of decreasing conflict and ensuring that each parent remains meaningfully involved in children's lives. Within a rebuttable equal parenting presumption, established cases of family violence would necessitate a different approach, in which a judicial determination of sole custody would be the likely outcome.

4 *Presumption against Equal Parenting Responsibility: Establish a rebuttable legal presumption against equal parenting in cases in*

which it is established that a child is in need of protection from a parent or parents. This presumption would develop clear and consistent guidelines for the legal determination of parenting after divorce in family violence and child abuse cases, consistent with those for children in two-parent families, using the safety of children as the paramount consideration. For some families, divorce will solve the problems that contributed to the violence; for others, the risk of abuse will be ongoing. This presumption does not equate to a presumption of no contact between the perpetrator and child in all cases where domestic violence is merely alleged (Hart and Bagshaw 2008; Jaffe, Lemon, and Poisson 2003); as in current practice, courts would make protective orders only when allegations are upheld. Equal parenting would be rebuttable only in cases of established violence or substantiated abuse; a judicial determination of sole custody or primary residence is warranted only with an investigated finding that a child is in need of protection from a parent. Finally, family violence and spousal abuse are criminal matters, and would be recognized as such in criminal law (Chisolm 2009; McIntosh and Chisolm 2009).

Thus, a legal presumption of equal parental responsibility would exclude cases of family violence established in criminal court, and cases of child abuse established via an investigated finding that a child is in need of protection. Family court judges, not trained in the finer points of child development and family dynamics, relying at times on imperfect third party assessments, are susceptible to making mistakes in determining the presence of violence and abuse, given the lax rules applied to fact-finding and perjury in family disputes (Bala 2000). Determining whether or not violence, a criminal act, has been perpetrated, and by whom, is a criminal court matter and not an appropriate role for the family court. An allegation of abuse is equivalent to neither a criminal conviction of abuse, nor a substantiated finding of abuse following an investigation by trained child protection authorities. In the absence of a criminal conviction or child protection finding, an equal parenting presumption ensures that children will have equal time with each parent, as opposed to being in the exclusive care and control of an abusive parent who has mounted the stronger case in a contested custody proceeding. In the family realm, when parties see themselves (and their children) to have been abused by the other, "victim politics" are commonplace. In such situations, if there is neither a criminal conviction nor a child-in-need-of-protection finding, equal parenting may be the most protective option for children. Detection of abuse is a difficult matter: at one extreme, a significant proportion of family violence situations are hidden to state authorities, and at the other extreme, false allegations are made. Where violence and abuse are alleged, criminal court proceedings as well as a comprehensive child welfare assessment must precede any family court judgment on matters related to parenting after divorce.

Pillar 2: Treatment: Divorce Education, Mediation, and Support/Intervention in High-Conflict Cases

Non-violent high-conflict couples can be helped with therapeutic interventions such as divorce education, family therapy, family mediation, and parenting coordination, and the passage of time, to achieve more amicable parenting arrangements (Kruk 1993a). As the dust settles and neither parent is threatened by the possible loss of one's children via a sole custody or primary residence order, it may be expected that parental conflict levels will naturally decline with the passage of time, as parents learn to separate their former spousal hostilities from their ongoing parenting responsibilities. Some parents will enter into a co-operative co-parenting routine, while others will fare better within a parallel parenting approach, in which their contact with each other is limited. Others will require support or specialized intervention to shield their children from their ongoing conflict.

Children's needs for protection from parental conflict must be addressed within any post-divorce parenting arrangement, and a full range of supports must be made available to parents in high conflict situations. Within these programs, children's needs become a means of connecting the parents in a positive manner at a time when conflict has divided them.

Divorce education   Given the lack of information available to divorcing families about what to do, what to expect, and the services available to them (Walker 1993), divorce education programs that make such information available prior to any dispute resolution process are vital. Parents who receive an orientation to the divorce process, and to the impact of divorce on family members, are better prepared for negotiation, mediation, and other non-adversarial dispute resolution alternatives, and are better able to keep the needs of their children at the forefront of their negotiations. Divorce education programs also offer a means to expose divorcing parties to mediation as an alternative mechanism for dispute resolution. Divorce educators with expertise in the expected effects of divorce on children and parents can be instrumental in helping parents recognize the potential psychological, social, and economic consequences of divorce and, on that foundation, promote parenting plans conducive to children maintaining meaningful, positive post-divorce relationships (Braver et al 1996).

A primary goal of divorce education programs is to focus on children's experiences of divorce and the disruption to a child's world that divorce may produce. Although for many adults divorce may herald an optimistic new "beginning," for children it is more likely to represent an unhappy "ending" of the family they know. When parents have a sound understanding of what the divorce experience means to a child, they will be in a better position to address that child's needs and support his or her adjustment to the consequences of divorce.

Parent education on children's needs and interests during and after the divorce transition, followed by therapeutic divorce mediation, offers an effective and efficient means of facilitating the development of co-operative parenting plans. Within such an approach, parent education may be used to introduce the option of equal or shared parenting as a viable alternative, and to reduce parents' anxiety about this new living arrangement. Mediation would then help parents work through the development of an equal or shared parenting plan, and the implementation of the plan in as co-operative a manner as possible. Specialized parent education programs have also been developed for high conflict couples (Grych 2005).

Family mediation   Mediation, as an alternative method of dispute resolution, has considerable (and as yet largely untapped) potential in establishing equal or shared parenting as the norm, rather than the exception, for divorced families. In the majority of non-violent high conflict cases, both parents are capable and loving caregivers and have at least the potential to minimize their conflict and co-operate with respect to their parenting responsibilities within an equal or shared parenting framework. There is strong empirical evidence that supports the use of mediation to settle complex, highly emotional disputes and reach agreements that are durable in post-divorce conflict. In public and private sectors, in voluntary and mandatory services, and when provided both early and late in the natural course of these disputes, family mediation has been consistently successful in resolving conflicts related to child custody and post-divorce parenting (Kelly 2004).

With a legal presumption of equal parental responsibility as the cornerstone, mediation could become the instrument whereby parents could be assisted in the development of a child-focused parenting plan. An educative approach should be an integral part of such a mediation process, with a primary focus on children's needs during and after the divorce process. A number of therapeutic family mediation models have been specifically developed for high conflict couples (Jacobs and Jaffe 2010; Kelly 2005; Kruk 1993a).

Combining divorce education with therapeutic family mediation has proven to be a highly effective method of intervention for highly conflicted parents. The process consists of four essential elements of a parent education program, and four phases of mediation (see Text Box 1).

Once a parenting plan is developed, parents may need the services of a mediator to assist in their ongoing parenting negotiations; they should be urged to return for mediation beyond a trial period as future issues develop or past difficulties re-emerge.

Text Box 1

A Framework for Divorce Education and Therapeutic Family Mediation for High Conflict Parents

PRE-MEDIATION: PARENT EDUCATION
1 Orientation to the divorce process and available services: stages of divorce/grieving; alternate dispute resolution processes (including mediation); post-divorce counselling services, and other community resources.
2 Children's needs and best interests in divorce.
3 Post-divorce equal and shared parenting alternatives.
4 Communication, negotiation, and problem-solving skills.

THERAPEUTIC FAMILY MEDIATION
1 Assessment to determine whether the parents are both ready to enter into therapeutic mediation, and whether equal or shared parenting is indicated.
2 Exploration of equal and shared parenting options and active promotion of a parenting plan that meets the children's needs.
3 Facilitation of negotiations toward the development of an individualized, co-operative parenting plan, which outlines specific living arrangements, schedules, roles, and responsibilities.
4 Continuing support/troubleshooting during the implementation of the parenting plan.

Post-divorce family therapy   Social institutional support for parents in the implementation of a parenting plan is critical, particularly for high-conflict cases in which children may be caught in the middle of disputes between parents. There are a number of existing models of therapeutic post-divorce support for such high-conflict families, including Garber's (2004) Direct

Co-parenting Intervention Model, Lebow's (2003) Integrative Family Therapy Model, and Taylor's (2005) CARE Model.

Of all the strategies that can be used by divorcing parents to reduce the harmful effects of divorce on their children, most important is the development and maintenance of a co-operative co-parenting relationship (Kruk 1993a; Garber 2004; Lebow 2003). Children's adjustment post-divorce in a long-term equal or shared parenting arrangement is facilitated by: a meaningful, routine relationship with each parent; an absence of hostile comments about the other parent; consistent, safe, structured, and predictable caregiving environments without parenting disruptions; healthy, caring, low-conflict relationships with each parent; and parents' emotional health and well-being (ibid). Any model of long-term support for high-conflict divorced families should focus on these factors to produce positive outcomes for children and their parents.

It is particularly important that hostility between parents be minimized following divorce. Currently, in cases in which there is ongoing litigation between parents, children are at greater risk of emotional damage than in less contentious circumstances; in many cases, divorce does not end marital conflict, but exacerbates it. It is important that children see the good qualities in both of their parents, and that parents work toward the development of positive relationships with each other. An effective support system is instrumental in providing parents with the necessary skills to deal with co-parenting challenges: "the central tenets of this system should be to reduce conflict, assure physical security, provide adequate support services to reduce harm to children, and to enable the family to manage its own affairs" (Wingspread Conference 2001, 147). In order for such a system to be successful, allied professionals need to be supportive of a model that helps resolve family disputes and focuses on the welfare of the children (ibid).

Six key considerations for a longer-term support model for high-conflict parents have been identified:

1 Whereas education on the impact of divorce on children both in the short and long term should be provided to parents

prior to the development of a parenting plan (Kruk 1993a; Lebow 2003), reinforcement and enhancement of pre-divorce education should take place in a structured format post-divorce (Kruk 1993a).

2 In addition to negotiating a workable parenting plan that meets the needs of children and delineates the responsibilities of parents, monitoring the consistency of the caregiving environments post-divorce is critical (Garber 2004).

3 Although Garber (2004) argues that direct contact between highly conflicted parents may be unnecessary in shared parenting, as parents can share parenting responsibilities within a parallel parenting arrangement, it seems clear that some form of intervention to mend the relationship between parents would contribute to the long-term success of the shared parenting arrangement (Lebow 2003). This intervention would focus on the development of positive interactions between family members, enhancing communication skills, developing a range of problem-solving skills, and enhancing non-aggressive negotiation skills.

4 Long-term counselling should be made available both to children alone, and to each parent and each child together, during and after divorce (Lebow 2003).

5 Long-term success of shared parenting is achieved through emotional healing post-divorce (Lebow 2003). Measures should be taken to allow each member of the family to gain an increased understanding and acceptance of the divorce as time goes by.

6 Finally, regular reviews of the parenting plan at pre-specified periods are useful during the implementation of the plan (Kruk 1993a). These reviews should take into consideration developmental changes in the children and their needs, as well as structural changes in the family such as the introduction of a new partner or step-parent, or relocation. The reviews should be conducted by a family mediator who can re-open the parenting plan for revision or modification as needed.

Parenting coordination   A relatively new intervention for high conflict parents unable to agree on parenting practices is that of parenting or dispute resolution coordination, which assists parents to settle post-divorce disputes, facilitates compliance with co-parenting plans and orders, and provides counselling, case management services, parent education, coaching, mediation, and arbitration of child-related conflicts as they arise. For example, a parenting coordinator may help parents to separate their previous marital hostilities from their ongoing parenting responsibilities. If striving for consistency in children's routines and in parenting styles escalates conflict, a parenting coordinator may focus parents on establishing consistent practices in their respective homes rather than engaging in repetitive unproductive negotiation.

Although empirical evidence of the effectiveness of parenting coordination is minimal, initial research results are encouraging (Firestone and Weinstein 2004; Coates et al 2004).

Parallel parenting For intractable high conflict situations, the option of parallel parenting exists, in which parents remain disengaged from each other as co-parents, and may assume decision-making responsibility in different domains (such as one parent being responsible for medical decisions and the other for education). Parallel parenting protects children from parental conflict while protecting their relationships with both parents. Such arrangements call for a high degree of specificity in the initial parenting plan, pre-empting the need for parents to communicate directly once the plan is in place. Many parents achieve co-operative parenting from a place of initial disengagement (Birnbaum and Fidler 2005).

Pillar 3: Prevention: Equal Parenting Public Education

Equal parenting education within the high school system, in marriage preparation courses, and upon divorce is an essential component of a more comprehensive program of parent education and support. Public education about various models of equal and shared parenting is especially important, including models for high conflict couples. Such programs are just beginning to be established, with an emphasis on including parents who have not traditionally been engaged by parenting support programs and services.

Equal parenting education should also involve the judiciary, as the effects of changes in family law on the actual practices of judges are uncertain, although there is evidence that the incidence of shared custody increases and sole maternal custody decreases after statutory changes that permit or encourage joint physical custody (Moyer 2004). The extent to which legislative reform can bring about the desired result will depend largely on the attitudes of the judiciary as well as legal practitioners. Assumptions about equal or shared parenting being unworkable in cases of disputed custody, and sole custody being in children's best interests in these cases, should be challenged, and stereotypes about parents in conflict addressed.

Engaging both the legal system and professional service providers in regard to the equal parenting presumption is another challenge. A constructive role for legal and/or family service providers needs to be advanced if family law is to remove itself from the adversarial arena in cases with no history of violence or abuse.

A large hurdle for non-resident parents and proponents of parenting-after-divorce law reform is garnering public and political attention and support to deal effectively with the social problems of fatherlessness, parental alienation, and diminished parental involvement in children's lives after divorce. These problems need to be made more visible, and constructive solutions advanced.

Pillar 4: Enforcement: Judicial Determination in Cases of Established Abuse and Enforcement of Equal Parental Responsibility Orders

The final pillar directly addresses the question of violence and abuse in family relationships, and enables sanctions to be imposed when there is non-compliance or repeated breaches of parenting orders. The recommendations of the 2007 Wingspread Conference on Domestic Violence and Family Courts (VerSteegh and Dalton 2008) are instructive in this regard.

When it comes to questions of family violence, children's and parents' safety must always be the primary consideration. Children's safety is best assured by addressing family violence as a criminal matter and child abuse as a child protection issue. Thus abuse and violence allegations must be fully investigated by child protection authorities and also prosecuted via criminal proceedings. At the same time, in criminal court it is important that innocence is presumed unless allegations are proven beyond a reasonable doubt. This is not always in line, however, with the practice of family courts in Canada, which often proceed as if alleged abuse has occurred even when not proven in criminal court, and in the absence of a child protection investigation; in child protection proceedings also, provincial family law allows child protection authorities to intervene on the basis of likelihood rather than incidence of abuse, via standardized risk assessments that lack an empirical foundation for their effectiveness as a child welfare methodology (Swift and Callahan 2011). Also, the allegation of conflict or violence is a powerful tool in the adversarial system, often resulting in the attenuation of contact between an accused parent and his or her children, which may place children at risk if the allegation is false (Birnbaum and Bala 2010; Sternberg 1997).

A rebuttable presumption of equal parental responsibility means that criminal court cases involving proven family violence would be subject to judicial determination of parenting after divorce, as children in such circumstances may be deemed as in need of protection as witnesses or victims of parental abuse. Those cases involving either a criminal conviction, such as assault, in a matter directly related to the parenting of the children, and a finding that a child is in need of protection from a parent by a statutory child welfare authority, would be followed by judicial determination of parenting after divorce. It may be appropriate in such cases, argue Jaffe et al (2005), for one or both parents to have limited or no contact with the children because of potential harm. It is my position, however, that parents should be considered innocent unless proven guilty, and that children's relationships with their parents need to be protected in the absence of a formal protection finding.

Family violence: separation of criminal and family law As former Canadian Minister of Justice Mark McGuigan noted in 1986, criminal and family law are fundamentally different arenas, and the criminal and family realms of law are best kept separate. Although a criminal conviction of assault against a family member would precipitate a child protection investigation, which may result in a finding that a child is in need of protection from a parent, family violence is a criminal matter and should be handled within that realm. It is noteworthy that substantiating allegations of abuse is highly problematic in child welfare proceedings, as opposed to proceeding with criminal prosecution (Cobley 2006). The objectives and nature of the proceedings of family and criminal court are fundamentally different: whereas establishing guilt and responsibility, and determining punishment, are key in criminal court, protection of children and their best interests are key in family court. Family law judges cannot adjudicate family violence, but family court should deal with child protection matters. In family court, the same procedures and protections should apply to all children, from divorced and non-divorced families alike, and children of divorce should receive the same protections that are afforded to children in non-divorced families, both in regard to being protected from an abusive parent in an abuse situation, and protected from being separated from a non-abusive parent.

In parenting-after-divorce situations in which assault is alleged, an informed and comprehensive, but expeditious, child welfare assessment is required. The criminal prosecution of family members alleged to have been violent toward any other member of the family would hold accountable both perpetrators and fabricators of violence. The family court would then retain its traditional role in the determination of legal parenting-after-divorce arrangements. In the context of family violence, the court may identify specific goals for the perpetrator of violence to achieve, with monitoring, before progressing toward the establishment of a co-parenting plan. Cases that would benefit from diversion to counselling could be referred to that arena.

Allegations of family violence should be part of a criminal and child protection process, not left to be settled in family court. The family court should not have to resolve conflicting criminal allegations, as litigants are entitled to more than "proof on the balance of probabilities" when their relationship with their children is at stake. The use of family courts as quasi-criminal courts that do not have the resources to apply due process when abuse allegations are made leaves judges susceptible to making wrong decisions, leading to potentially greater harm to children. Women's advocates have long argued that the adversarial system does not protect abused women adequately, and men's advocates are beginning to identify the ineffectiveness of the courts in dealing with the abuse of men. Detection of genuine abuse cases is a difficult yet critical matter, and strengthening current child protection and criminal prosecution responses to these cases will require refining the ability to discern abuse where it exists, as well as dealing effectively with unproven allegations. When abuse allegations are made, a competent child welfare authority must undertake an immediate and thorough investigation of the allegations. Child exposure to spousal violence should be a legal basis for finding a child in need of protection.

In non-abusive and non-violent situations, when there is no finding that a child is in need of protection from a parent, to the degree that the adversarial sole custody system disregards children's need for both parents in their lives, it exacerbates the negative consequences of divorce for children not exposed to family violence or abuse. Children need to know that their relationships with each of their parents are protected. If one parent is undermined or denigrated, so is the child. The loss of a loving parent through divorce has devastating consequences for children's self-concept and physical, psychological, and emotional well-being. Children who are the innocent victims of custody wars between parents, and of the social institutions and policies that exacerbate the conflict, are a highly vulnerable and overlooked population.

When equal or shared parenting arrangements are legally ordered and a parent refuses to abide by the order, disrupting the other parent's time with the children, enforcement measures may be required. Wherever possible, however, mediation should be encouraged in cases in which equal or shared parenting orders are breached. Models such as Manitoba's access assistance program, piloted from 1989 to 1993 to facilitate the exercise of access, could be modified for use in dealing with equal and shared parenting orders. It is expected, however, that breaches are less likely when both parents have an active role to play in children's lives within a shared custody arrangement.

When enforcement measures are necessary to ensure compliance with equal parenting orders, solutions may involve temporary reduction or loss of parenting time, or the following sanctions:

1 a requirement that a parent comply with "make-up" contact if contact has been missed through a breach of an order;
2 a discretionary requirement to pay compensation for reasonable expenses incurred due to a breach of an order;
3 a requirement to pay legal costs against the party that has breached the order; and
4 a discretionary imposition of a bond for all breaches of orders.

9

Specific Challenges and Recommendations

In addition to the provision of support programs to facilitate the development of parenting plans and ongoing services to ensure their success, particularly for high conflict families, there are a number of linked issues that must be considered if equal parenting is to be a realistic objective for the majority of families in conflict upon divorce. Many of these issues are the fallout of the present adversarial winner-take-all sole custody system, and are discussed briefly in this chapter as specific challenges to be overcome and as additional recommendations to the four-pillar approach discussed in chapter 8. These include post-traumatic stress among disenfranchised parents, parental alienation and reunification, false allegations and false denials, child support, and relocation. The topics of stepfamily divorce, same-sex parents, assisted reproduction, and new reproductive technologies are also examined.

DISENFRANCHISED PARENTS
AND POST-TRAUMATIC STRESS

Children and parents who have undergone abuse, including the "legal abuse" of parents who have been disenfranchised from their children's lives subsequent to sole custody and primary residence judgments (Kruk 2010a), are subject to post-traumatic stress. Support services, largely lacking during and after the divorce transition, are urgently needed for children and parents who have been affected. In addition, non-resident parents have been subject to shame and stigma, lack of access to their children (including the lack of access enforcement), barriers imposed by the court system, and devaluation of their role as parents. Those who speak about the pain in their lives and their feelings of being emotionally wounded are subjected to a mean-spirited cultural response, in which all talk of emotional wounds is mocked (ibid).

Engaging non-resident and disenfranchised fathers in particular is a significant challenge; clinical and research literature has described the lack of "fit" between fathers and therapeutic agents as emanating from two sources: the characteristics of men and fathers themselves (their resistance to counselling and therapy), and aspects of the therapeutic process (which have failed to successfully engage fathers). Patterns of traditional gender-role socialization directing men toward self-sufficiency and control, independent problem-solving, and emotional restraint have largely worked against fathers' ability to acknowledge personal difficulties and request help. A fear of self-disclosure and a feeling of disloyalty to one's family in exposing family problems are not uncommon; a fear of losing control over one's life and a need to present an image of control or a "facade of coping" in the form of exterior calm, strength, and rationality, despite considerable inner turmoil, characterize many fathers. Professional service providers do not always consider such psychological obstacles to therapy and thus do not address fathers' unique needs. The research on divorced fathers is clear about their most pressing need: their continued meaningful involvement with their children, as active parents. The lack of recognition of this primary need is the main reason for therapists' lack of success in engaging divorced fathers.

Above all, the key to engaging disenfranchised parents is to validate their parental identity, and to combine advocacy efforts with counselling focused on enhancing their role as active and responsible parents. Social workers and other human service professionals have been notably absent in the politics of reform with respect to the legal determination of parenting after divorce, and are desperately needed as allies in policy reform efforts. The best way to support disenfranchised parents is through such advocacy and activism, breaking apart the custodial/noncustodial and residential/non-residential parent dichotomy, and advancing the cause of equal parenting.

An active program of outreach is essential, as disenfranchised fathers and mothers report a lack of helpful support services, and they remain a highly vulnerable population (Kruk 2010a; Kruk 2010b). Service providers need to be persistent and proactive, as it takes time to build and sustain engagement in the context of these parents' feelings of isolation, alienation, or helplessness, and their tendency to wait until there is a crisis before accessing support. Parents who were highly involved with and attached to their children and suddenly find themselves forcefully removed from their children's lives experience trauma writ large. The experience of being removed as a loving parent from the life of one's child via a sole custody order strikes at the heart of one's being. As discussed earlier, high rates of depression and suicide are endemic among parents disenfranchised from their children's lives, particularly when parents feel unsupported and victimized by judicial and legal systems. Being vigilant regarding symptoms of post-traumatic stress and suicidal ideation among non-resident fathers and mothers is an essential role for service providers. A strengths-based approach, recognizing non-resident parents' aspirations to their children's well-being, and the experience, knowledge, and skills that they can contribute to this well-being, is a vital role for professional service providers.

PARENTAL ALIENATION AND REUNIFICATION

Most non-resident parents who have become disengaged from their children's lives have lost contact involuntarily (many as a result of parental alienation), and are looking for constructive alternatives to adversarial methods of reconnecting with their children. Parental alienation, in the context of a sole custody or primary residence order, involves the "programming" of a child by one parent to denigrate the other parent, and is a sign of a parent's inability to separate from the couple conflict and focus on the needs of the child. Such denigration of the non-resident parent by the custodial parent, resulting in a child's emotional rejection of the non-resident parent, results in the loss of a capable and loving parent from the life of a child. Parental alienation is more common than is often assumed: Bala et al (2010) report both an increasing incidence and increased judicial findings of parental alienation; Fidler and Bala (2010) report estimates of parental alienation in 11–15% of divorces involving children; Bernet et al (2010) estimate that about 1% of children and adolescents in North America experience parental alienation.

There is now scholarly consensus that severe alienation is abusive to children (Fidler and Bala 2010), although a neglected form of child abuse (Bernet et al 2010), as divorce practitioners are largely unaware of or minimize the extent of the phenomenon. As reported by adult children of divorce, alienating parents use a variety of tactics which are tantamount to extreme psychological maltreatment of children, including spurning, terrorizing, isolating, corrupting, exploiting, and denying emotional responsiveness (Baker 2010). For the child, parental alienation is a serious mental condition, based on a false belief that the alienated parent is a dangerous and unworthy parent. The severe effects of parental alienation on children are well-documented: low self esteem and self-hatred, lack of trust, depression, substance abuse, and other forms of addiction are widespread (Baker 2005) as children lose the capacity to give and accept love from a parent (Warshak 2010a). Self-hatred is particularly disturbing among affected children, as children internalize the hatred targeted toward the alienated parent, are led to believe that the alienated parent did not love or want them, and experience severe guilt related to betraying the alienated parent (Baker 2005). Their depression is rooted in feelings of being unloved by one of their parents, and in their separation from that parent while being denied the opportunity to mourn the loss of the parent, or to even talk about the parent (ibid). Alienated children typically have conflicted or distant relationships with the alienating parent also, and are at high risk of becoming alienated from their own children; Baker (2005) reports that fully half of the respondents in her study of adult children who had experienced alienation as children were alienated from their own children.

Children and parents who have undergone forced separation from each other in the absence of abuse, including cases of parental alienation, are highly subject to post-traumatic stress, and reunification efforts in these cases should proceed carefully and with sensitivity. Research has shown that many alienated children can transform quickly from refusing or staunchly resisting the rejected parent to being able to show and receive love from that parent, followed by an equally swift shift back to the alienated position when back in the orbit of the alienating parent (Fidler and Bala 2010). Alienated children seem to have a secret wish for someone to call their bluff, compelling them to reconnect with the parent they claim to hate (Baker 2005). Thus, while children's stated wishes regarding parental contact in contested parenting after divorce should be considered, they should not be determinative, especially in suspected cases of alienation.

Reunification programs subsequent to prolonged absence should be undertaken with service providers with specialized expertise in parental alienation reunification. A number of intervention models have been developed, the best-known being Warshak's (2010b) Family Bridges Program, an educative and experiential program focused on multiple goals: allowing the child to have a healthy relationship with both parents, removing the child from parental conflict, and encouraging child autonomy, multiple perspective-taking, and critical thinking. Sullivan's Overcoming Barriers Family Camp (Sullivan, Ward, and Deutsch 2010), which combines psycho-educational and clinical intervention within an environment of "milieu therapy," is aimed toward the development of an agreement regarding the sharing of parenting time, and a written aftercare plan. Friedlander and Walters's (2010) Multimodal Family Intervention provides different interventions for situations of parental alignment, alienation, enmeshment, and estrangement. All of these programs emphasize the clinical significance and utmost importance of regarding both parents as equally valued in the child's eyes in reunification efforts subsequent to parental alienation. At the same time, these programs help enmeshed children relinquish their protective role toward their alienating parents.

In reunification programs, alienated parents will benefit from guidelines with respect to their efforts to provide a safe, comfortable, open, and inviting atmosphere for their children. Ellis (2005) outlines five strategies for alienated parents: (1) erode children's negative image by providing incongruent information; (2) refrain from actions that put the child in the middle of conflict; (3) consider ways to mollify the anger and hurt of the alienating parent; (4) look for ways to dismantle the coalition between the child and alienating parent and convert enemies to allies; and (5) never give up on reunification efforts. As much as possible, however, Warshak (2010a) recommends that alienated parents arrange for their children to see third parties treating the parent with high regard, to let the children understand that their negative opinion, and the opinion of the other parent, is not shared by the rest of the world. This type of experience will leave a stronger impression than anything the alienated parent can say on his or her own behalf.

With alienating parents, it is important to emphasize that as responsible parenting involves respecting the other parent's role in the child's life, any form of denigration of a former partner and co-parent is harmful to children. Children's connections to each parent must be respected to ensure their well-being. Alienating parents are themselves emotionally fragile, often enmeshed with the child, with a sense of entitlement, needing to maintain control (Richardson 2006), and pose significant clinical challenges. Poisoning minds and instilling hatred toward a parent are forms of abuse of children, as hatred of a parent is not an emotion that comes naturally to a child; it has to be taught. When children grow up in an atmosphere of parental alienation, their primary role model is a maladaptive, dysfunctional parent. Although some commentators (Fidler and Bala 2010) recommend custody reversal in such cases, or at least a period of separation between a child and an alienating parent during the reunification process with an alienated parent, it is generally agreed that a non-punitive approach is most effective, engaging and involving the alienating parent in reunification programs whenever possible (Kelly 2010; Sullivan, Ward, and Deutsch 2010). Equal or shared parenting is clearly preferable to sole custody in potential alienation cases, as courts are ill-equipped to detect potential alienation and, as discussed in chapter 7, equal parenting is preventive of alienation.

In regard to parental alienation, the system is the problem; that is, the roots of alienation lie primarily in the adversarial nature of legal determination of parenting after divorce. Parents are set up to fight in an effort to win primary residence or custody of their children, and the system rewards those skilled in adversarial combat. Parents often win their case by disparaging the other parent as a parent, in effect engaging in alienating behaviour, and alienating behaviour is thereby encouraged. A rebuttable legal presumption of equal parenting is the most effective means of combating parental alienation and its consequences.

FALSE ALLEGATIONS AND FALSE DENIALS

It is not uncommon for spouses in high-conflict divorces to make false or exaggerated allegations of abuse, and false denials are equally a problem. Allegations of parental abuse or neglect of children should be investigated in a timely manner, and allegations of family violence dealt with as a criminal matter in criminal court. False allegations are a serious matter, both in the harms resulting to individual children and accused parents, but also in the fact that a proliferation of such allegations results in the trivialization of family violence, as parents and children who are genuine victims of abuse are often not believed.

When an allegation of abuse is made and an acquittal results in criminal court, this should be binding on a judge in any subsequent family law proceeding. If an accused is convicted in a criminal trial, however, the judge in a family law trial must take the criminal conviction as conclusive evidence that the abuse in question occurred, and act accordingly. The outright suspension of parental involvement in a child's life, however, must be done only in the case of established child abuse and, even then, reestablishment of a positive parent-child relationship must remain a goal.

CHILD SUPPORT

Although financial child support is not the focus of this book, it is an essential need of children and a responsibility of parents. Child custody is closely related to child support and family maintenance.

The economic independence of parents is a goal that proponents of equal pay for work of equal value, and those challenging occupational segregation and wage differentials, have advanced. Such a goal is highly compatible with an equal- or shared-parental-responsibility approach to parenting after divorce. Shared parental responsibility for both child care and child support, in the context of both parents working outside the home while actively parenting, is an important principle to uphold. Both parenting and paid work should be recognized as work of equal value.

In Canada, current federal child support guidelines have been structured around the traditional arrangement of sole custody or primary residence with one parent, in which the calculation of child support obligations is based on the income of the non-custodial parent. The guidelines allow for a deviation from the specified amounts in the event of shared custody; that is, when a child lives with each parent at least 40% of the time. An equal- or shared-parental-responsibility framework would mean that this exception to the guidelines would become the norm for parenting arrangements, which would necessitate a modification of the guidelines. The guidelines would need to take both parents' incomes into account, and would have to be based on a formula different to that which currently exists.

Although the economic consequences of divorce for all family members are devastating, the recent finding that the standard of living of non-custodial parents falls below that of custodial parents (Braver and Stockberger 2005) is largely unrecognized, and this is a cause for concern, as child support guidelines are based not only on a sole custody framework but also on the feminization of poverty thesis. New child support guidelines within an equal or shared parenting approach should aim toward equalizing the standard of living of both households. In addition, greater attention should be paid to the general lack of government-funded support for parenting itself, and the problem of wage differentials between the genders.

In regard to child support enforcement, there is no evidence that the recent trend of stricter government enforcement of child support obligations has solved the economic difficulties faced by families of divorce. Millar (2010), describing the emergence of imprisonment as a new strategy in the collection of child-support debt, found that Aboriginals, visible minorities, the unemployed, and those without post-secondary education are over-represented among those imprisoned, concluding that child support enforcement as an implement of social policy pushes families further into poverty, especially in the case of low-income payers.

RELOCATION

Parenting plans that both accommodate parental relocation and maintain the same proportion of residential parental responsibility being exercised by each parent before and after relocation, should be encouraged. Although equal or shared parenting can be made to work when parents live some distance apart, particularly with older children, children's relationships with both parents are best safeguarded by legislation that discourages child relocation when both parents are actively involved in parenting after divorce. New legislation in Wisconsin, for example, requires a moving parent to prove that prohibiting the move would be harmful to children's best interests. In contested cases, a rebuttable presumption that children remain in the community in which they have become adjusted would safeguard children's existing relationships and should be part of equal parenting legislation.

STEPFAMILY DIVORCE

In cases in which a biological parent is the primary caregiver of children in a stepfamily, special consideration should be given to the unique nature of the biological parent-child relationship in the legal determination of parenting after divorce. However, the individualized four-step equal parenting presumption outlined in chapter 8, with an expectation that a parenting plan be developed by the parents, followed by application of the approximation rule, with equal parental time applied in cases in which both partners were primary caregivers before the divorce, would apply equally to stepfamilies who are in the process of divorce.

SAME-SEX PARENTS

Although the proportion of same-sex partnerships is quite small, now constituting 0.6% of all couple families in Canada, with only 9% of these couples having children living with them (Vanier Institute for the Family 2010), the struggles experienced by same-sex parents in conflict over post-divorce parenting arrangements are similar to those in heterosexual families. Same-sex parents are often raising children from former heterosexual unions of one of the partners in circumstances very much like a heterosexual step-parent family. And although discrimination against gay and lesbian parents with respect to parenting after divorce has long been an issue of concern, this seems be have abated in Canada in recent years.

Approximately 15% of lesbian couples are raising children as compared to only 3% of male couples. However, a norm in both gay and lesbian families is that of an egalitarian division of labour with respect to child care responsibilities (ibid). The equal parenting presumption proposed here would thus apply in cases of child custody dispute in gay and lesbian families.

Same-sex couples may have children via several different routes, including adoption, surrogacy, and sperm donation, as well as bringing children into a relationship from a former heterosexual union. In circumstances in which gay and lesbian parents were raising children from former heterosexual unions of one of the partners, and child care responsibilities are shared between the biological parents and the step-parent, in the interests of children maintaining existing attachments, reducing inter-parental conflict, and ensuring stability and continuity in children's routines, these arrangements should continue after the divorce of the same-sex partners. Custody contests between same-sex parents are just as acrimonious and damaging to children within a sole custody regime as those between heterosexual parents. Although some in the gay and lesbian community have argued that special consideration be given to the importance of the biological parent-child relationship, with a "presumption in favour of the natural" being applied (Somerville 2006), there is no reason that same-sex partnerships should be treated any differently from other stepfamilies. The individualized four-step equal parenting presumption, with an expectation that a parenting plan be developed by the parents, followed by application of the approximation rule, with equal parental time applied in cases in which both partners were primary caregivers before the divorce, would apply equally well to same-sex families who are in the process of divorce.

ASSISTED REPRODUCTION AND NEW REPRODUCTIVE TECHNOLOGIES

Legislatures in Canada and abroad are just beginning to grapple with amending parentage and parenting-after-divorce/child custody laws in situations of assisted conception, including sperm donation. Similar to the debate regarding closed versus open adoption respecting children's need for identity and the right to know their biological parents, the issue of children's interests vis-à-vis knowledge of their biological parents within the assisted reproduction, and new reproductive technologies arena is far from resolved. Although the resolution of such ethical issues is beyond the scope of this book, a child-focused perspective is largely missing in current debates about parentage, assisted reproduction, and new reproductive technologies, and needs to be placed front and centre in the discussion. Similarly, in the case of same-sex couples who are claiming that the law which prohibits certain uses of new reproductive technologies is unconstitutional because it infringes upon their rights to found a family in the ways they wish, including cloning and paid surrogate motherhood, the perspective and interests of the resulting child have been largely left unconsidered. As Somerville (2006) notes, "non-natural" birth children may feel a profound loss of identity because they do not know their natural parents, and this harm may represent a breach of ethics on the part of parents and any society that allows such procedures.

10

Conclusion

In stating the case for the institution of a rebuttable legal presumption of equal parental responsibility in situations of contested parenting after divorce, I have aimed toward clarifying the current state of knowledge on the matter of the best interests of the child in the divorce transition. The arguments I make rest upon the principle that the needs and interests of children should be the paramount consideration in the legal arena, and on the fact that these best interests need to be clearly defined and based on available research evidence regarding the most important factors associated with children's well-being after divorce, and applied to children's and families' individual circumstances, rather than being based on judicial discretion. The challenge has been to develop and establish a legal presumption that minimizes judicial discretion, enhances determinacy, and reduces litigation, while at the same time serving the best interests of the child and taking into account each child's and family's unique circumstances.

There is now a general consensus within the research community that neither the discretionary best-interests-of-the-child standard nor sole custody or primary residence orders are serving the needs of children and families of divorce. The destructiveness of the winner-take-all adversarial system and consequences of litigation on child and family well-being cannot be overstated. The vagueness and indeterminacy of an undefined best-interests-of-the-child standard gives unfettered discretion to judges not trained in child development and family dynamics, resulting in unpredictable and inconsistent outcomes based on idiosyncratic biases and subjective, value-based judgments, fuelling parental conflict and increasing litigation in cases in which parents are unable to agree on parenting arrangements. The damaging effects of parental removal from children's lives, including father absence, are thoroughly documented. Parents should be the pride of their children; when a capable and loving parent is diminished in the eyes of a child by being removed as a custodial parent, the effects are profound and far-reaching.

A child-focused approach to the legal determination of parenting after divorce is needed to reduce harm to children in the divorce transition and to ensure their well-being. The well-being of children should take precedence over judicial biases and preferences, professional self-interest, gender politics, the desire of a parent to remove the other from the child's life, and the wishes of a parent who is found to be a danger to the child. It is in children's interests that any new legal paradigm relating to parenting after divorce must: ensure consistency in decision-making, removing discretion in areas in which judges have no formal expertise; protect children from the loss of a primary parent, preserving loving parent-child relationships; protect children from violence and abuse, and ongoing high conflict; and ensure stability and continuity in children's routines and living arrangements. The rebuttable legal equal-parental-responsibility presumption outlined in this book offers the best hope for accomplishing these goals.

The equal-parenting-responsibility presumption represents a viable, child-focused alternative to the discretionary best-interests-of-the-child/sole custody approach. The presumption builds upon the emerging consensus in support of equal parenting, both within the scholarly community and among the public. It is also based on the standard of the best interests of the child from the perspective of the child, on what children themselves have identified as serving their best interests. It prioritizes a responsibility-to-needs orientation over a rights-based approach, taking into account parents' views on the needs of their children, and parental and social institutional responsibilities to those needs. It is a strengths-based approach, which recognizes parental strengths rather than focusing on their individual limitations, which tends to be the focus of a litigation process.

Above all else, the equal parental presumption addresses the primary need of children in the divorce transition: the preservation of existing nurturing parent-child attachments for the majority of children and families in conflict. It ensures the active involvement of both parents in children's everyday lives and routines, including bedtime and waking rituals, transitions to and from school, extracurricular and recreational activities, and significant time during the school week – all critical to children's well-being.

The literature does not support the presumption that equal parental responsibility is contraindicated in cases of high conflict, and thus high conflict should not be used to justify restrictions on children's contact with either of their parents. The equal-parenting-responsibility presumption is associated with diminished conflict between parents after divorce, as neither parent is threatened by the potential loss of his or her children, and is preventive of first-time separation-initiated violence endemic to ongoing child custody conflict.

The equal-parental-responsibility presumption also leads to predictability of outcome, a reduction in litigation, and an incentive for mediation and the development of parenting plans. Currently courts are the default option when parents are at an impasse regarding post-divorce parenting arrangements; other methods of dispute resolution may be used only by mutual consent of the parties. When one party in dispute perceives an advantage in going to court, that is the venue where the dispute will end up; and when the legal system consistently favours one side in a dispute (Millar 2009), that party has little incentive to attempt non-adversarial means of resolution. There is also little that mediation or "collaborative law" can do to mitigate the bias of the court system. Further, the "divorce industry" contains a myriad of players, judges and lawyers, child counsellors and psychologists, custody assessors, forensic accountants and pension evaluators, social workers, police officers, and all of their support staff who collectively represent a constituency of beneficiaries who defend the status quo. The equal parenting presumption reverses this state of affairs, removing the need for court involvement and judicial indeterminacy from the parenting-after-divorce and divorce arena in all but family violence and abuse cases.

The scientific community is now in a position to draw conclusions regarding the amount of parenting time necessary to achieve child well-being and positive outcomes, with an emerging consensus among divorce researchers that a minimum of one-third time with each parent is necessary to achieve child well-being, with additional benefits accruing up to and including equal 50–50 time (Fabricius et al 2010). Equal parenting is based on strong research evidence that the continuity of relationships with parents and extended family is of paramount importance to children of divorce, that divorce is primarily a parental responsibility, and that the state should play a facilitative role by ensuring a level playing field, and making an already painful process as humane, efficient, and inexpensive as possible. In my view, each of the sixteen arguments presented in favour of the equal parenting presumption (see chapter 7) is sufficient to warrant replacing the discretionary best-interests-of-the-child standard with equal parenting; combined, they are a powerful testament to the urgent need for law reform toward the implementation of true equal parenting.

The equal parental responsibility approach detailed in chapter 8 is unique, and represents an evolution from the best-interests-of-the-child standard, the primary caregiver presumption, the parenting plan approach, the approximation rule, and joint-legal-custody arrangements. Although it is first and foremost a child-focused framework based on current empirical research findings, it also addresses the primary concerns of both mothers' and fathers' groups in regard to the legal determination of parenting after divorce. The equal-parental-responsibility presumption outlined here is, essentially, a hybrid of the approximation rule and a joint physical custody presumption. It also combines a rebuttable legal presumption of equal parental responsibility with a rebuttable presumption against equal parental responsibility in established cases of family violence and child abuse, along with a legal requirement that family violence allegations be fully investigated in a timely manner, and family violence treated as a criminal act, with a corresponding finding made that any affected children are in need of protection. In replacing the best-interests-of-the-child standard with the child-in-need-of-protection standard in cases of family violence and child abuse, it affirms the right of children to know and be cared for by both of their parents, regardless of parental status, and the right of children to be equally protected from parental abuse. The proposed framework of equal parental responsibility is thus highly individualized and tailored to the unique situation and circumstances of each child and family, as there is no definitive parenting arrangement that can protect all children from the negative consequences of parental divorce.

For an equal-parental-responsibility presumption to work, supports need to be in place to ensure its success, including divorce education programs, therapeutic family mediation, parenting coordination, and other specialized programs for high conflict families. These services must be an essential part of equal-parental-responsibility legislation, as does a comprehensive system of equal parenting public education.

Given the overwhelming research evidence and public support in favour of an equal-parental-responsibility presumption, its characterization by divorce industry professionals as an outlandish proposition and an arrogant presumption of extremist elements is no longer valid. It is time, proponents believe, to break down the roadblocks to the passage of equal-parental-responsibility legislation around the globe. However, if the more stringent child-in-need-of-protection standard were to replace the best-interests-of-the-child standard in regard to the removal of a parent from a child's life after divorce, the livelihood of family-law and allied professionals would be seriously threatened. Even more of a threat would be the curtailment of the power of lawyers and judges in the realm of parenting after divorce – that is the real issue, the primary barrier to meaningful parenting-after-divorce law reform, according to some. The real answer, however, is likely a little more complex. Human-services providers are motivated not only by self-interest, but also by altruistic motives, seeking to make a positive difference in the lives of vulnerable children and families. The well-being of children is the primary motive of most practitioners and policymakers in the field of parenting after divorce. The road to hell, however, is paved with good intentions, and a more considered examination of alternative approaches to helping children and families in post-divorce transition is now warranted. Equal parental responsibility as a legal presumption is primary among these alternatives. The "parental deficit" perspective prevalent among many divorce practitioners, I would argue, is a significant barrier to the establishment of an equal-parental-responsibility presumption, and deflects attention and accountability away from social institutions and their responsibility to support parents. A strengths-based orientation, on the other hand, emphasizes the importance of protecting primary relationships and strengthening children's emotional security in their relationships with both their parents, reducing parental conflict and litigation, ensuring stability and continuity in children's lives, allowing for predictability of outcome, and simplifying and expediting the legal determination of parenting after divorce as fundamental to children's well-being. An equal-parental-responsibility presumption makes this ideal possible.

The lack of an equal-parental-responsibility presumption is one manifestation of the lack of responsibility of social institutions to support parents in the fulfillment of their responsibilities to their children. The disappearance of parents from children's lives in Western nations is the direct result of child and family policies that serve to disconnect children from the active involvement of their parents in their lives (Kruk 2011). Western child care, child custody, and child protection policies and systems represent significant barriers to parental involvement in children's lives. Present-day child custody policies remove non-custodial and non-resident divorced parents from the daily routines of children's lives, just as child care policies lessen direct parental involvement, as children spend less time in their parents' care and more time in non-parental care. Also, child protection policies emphasize child removal over family preservation and discourage ongoing parental contact and family reunification. The cumulative effect of these policies is a significant overall reduction in parental time with children.

As Canada lags behind other countries in parental involvement levels, there is an urgent need for policy recognition that children need both parents and that parents require social supports to address children's needs for parents' active and responsible involvement in children's lives. Relative to children in other economically advanced nations, Canadian children score high on behavioural and risk measures such as substance abuse, violence and risk-taking (UNICEF 2007; UNICEF 2013). In regard to subjective well-being, Canadian children rank very low; the rate of youth suicide and depression in Canadian children is of particular concern. Poverty of parental involvement is central to the compromised physical, psychological, and emotional well-being of children in Canada and globally. Equal parental responsibility is a core element of a broader initiative to promote a "presumption in favour of the natural" (Somerville 2006) in child and family policy. Responsible parental involvement in children's lives before and after divorce is the integral element of an equal parenting presumption, and a part of a broader initiative favouring the return of the "natural parent" in Canadian law.

We should heed Bauserman's (2012) cautionary note about the need for further research on parental adjustment to divorce, particularly in regard to child-related conflict and its resolution. It is ironic that the "friendly parent" rule has come under increased criticism and scrutiny, even though its antithesis, the mean-spirited parent, is never considered. A friendly parent is one who is not threatened by equality of parenting time within the existing child custody system, as he or she will exert an equal influence in a child's life. Children need both parents, to the fullest extent possible, if they are to develop to an optimal degree.

If children are loved, taught, and cared for with the honour and respect they are entitled to as human beings, and their needs are addressed by responsible adults, they will mature into responsible, loving, and kind adults. It is incumbent upon those working within political, social welfare, judicial, and child protection systems to support parents in learning about how to raise children in a wholesome way, without teaching them greed, hatred, and ignorance.

The invisible victims of parental disengagement from children's lives are children. This book has examined children's needs and parental responsibilities in parenting after divorce, and the support parents need to enable them to address their children's needs. The book has focused on clarifying what the research says in regard to the best interests of children from a child-focused perspective. In sum, children need both parents and social policies that promote parental involvement in children's lives. A legal equal parenting presumption for children of divorce and their families is pivotal to the realization of this ideal.

Bibliography

Allen, Douglas, and Margaret Brinig. 2011. "Do Joint Parenting Laws Make Any Difference?" *Journal of Empirical Legal Studies* 8 (2): 304–24.

Amato, Paul. 2000. "The Consequences of Divorce for Adults and Children." *Journal of Marriage and the Family* 62: 1269–87.

Amato, Paul R. and Cassandra Dorius. 2012. "Fathers, Children, and Divorce." In *The Role of the Father in Child Development*, edited by Michael Lamb, 177–201. New York: John Wiley and Sons.

Amato, Paul R. and Joan G. Gilbreth. 1999. "Non Father-Resident Fathers and Children's Well Being: A Meta-Analysis." *Journal of Marriage and the Family* 61: 557–73.

Amato, Paul R. and Bruce Keith. 1991. "Parental Divorce and the Well-Being of Children: A Meta-Analysis." *Psychological Bulletin* 110: 26–46.

Amato, Paul R., Catherine Meyers, and Robert Emery. 2009. "Changes in Nonresident Father-Child Contact from 1976 to 2002." *Family Relations* 58: 41–53.

American Bar Association. 2010. "Review of the Year in Family Law: Custody Criteria." *Family Law Quarterly* 43 (4): 973–4.

Aquilino, William S. 2010. "Noncustodial Father Child Relationship from Adolescence into Young Adulthood." *Journal of Marriage and Family* 68: 929–45.

Archer, John. 2000. "Sex Differences in Aggression Acts Between Heterosexual Partners: A Meta-analytic Review." *Psychological Bulletin*, 126 (5): 651–80.

– 2002. "Sex Differences in Physically Aggressive Acts Between Heterosexual Partners: A Meta-analytic Review." *Aggression and Violent Behavior* 7: 213–351.

Arditti, Joyce A., and Anne Prouty. 1999. "Change, Disengagement, and Renewal: Relationship Dynamics Between Young Adults with Divorced Parents and Their Fathers." *Journal of Marriage and Family Therapy* 25: 61–81.

Atwood, Barbara Ann. 2007. "Comment on Warshak: The Approximation Rule As a Work in Progress." *American Journal of Family Therapy*, 1 (2): 126–8.

Baker, Amy. 2005. "Long-Term Effects of Parental Alienation on Adult Children." *American Journal of Family Therapy* 33: 289–302.

– 2010. "Adult Recall of Parental Alienation in a Community Sample: Prevalence and Associations with Psychological Maltreatment." *Journal of Divorce and Remarriage* 51: 16–35.

Bala, Nicholas. 2000. *The Best Interests of the Child in the Post-modern Era: A Central But Paradoxical Concept*. Paper Presentation at the Law Society of Canada, Special Lectures 2000, Osgoode Hall, Toronto.

Bala, Nicholas, Suzanne Hunt, and Carolyn McCarney. 2010. "Parental Alienation: Canadian Court Cases 1989–2008." *Family Court Review* 48 (1): 164–79.

Bala, Nicholas, Peter Jaffe, and Claire Crooks. 2007. *Spousal Violence and Child-Related Cases: Challenging Cases Requiring Differentiated Responses*. Paper Presentation at the Ontario Court of Justice, Judicial Development Institute, Toronto.

Baskerville, Stephen. 2007. *Taken Into Custody*. Nashville: Cumberland House.

Bauserman, Robert. 2002. "Child Adjustment in Joint Custody Versus Sole Custody Arrangements: A Meta-analytic Review." *Journal of Family Psychology*, 16: 91–102.

– 2012. "A Meta-analysis of Parental Satisfaction, Adjustment, and Conflict in Joint Custody and Sole Custody Following Divorce." *Journal of Divorce and Remarriage* 53: 464–88.

Bender, William N. 1994. "Joint Custody: The Option of Choice." *Journal of Divorce and Remarriage* 21 (3/4): 115–31.

Benjamin, Michael and Howard H. Irving. 1989. "Shared Parenting: A Critical Review of the Research Literature." *Family and Conciliation Courts Review* 27: 21–35.

Berg, Ellen. 2003. "Effects of Closeness to Custodial Parents and Nonresident Parents on Adolescent Self Esteem." *Journal of Divorce and Remarriage* 40: 69–86.

Berger, Lawrence M., Patricia Brown, Eunhee Joung, Marygold Melli, and Lynn Wimer. 2008. "The Stability of Child Physical Placements Following Divorce: Descriptive Evidence from Wisconsin." *Journal of Marriage and Family* 70: 273–83.

Bernet, William, Wilfrid Von Boch-Galhau, Amy Baker, and Stephen L. Morrison. 2010. "Parental Alienation, DSM-V, and ICD–11." *American Journal of Family Therapy* 38: 76–187.

Bessner, Ronda. 2002. The *Voice of the Child in Divorce, Custody, and Access Proceedings*. Ottawa: Department of Justice Canada.

Bianchi, Suzanne. 2000. "Maternal Employment and Time with Children." *Demography* 37: 401–14.

Bianchi, Suzanne, John Robinson, and Melissa Milkie. 2006. *Changing Rhythms of the American Family*. New York: Sage.

Biller, Henry. 1993. *Fathers and Families*. Westport, CT: Auburn House.

Birnbaum, Rachel and Nicholas Bala. 2010. "Differentiating High Conflict Cases." *Family Court Review* 48 (3): 403–16.

Birnbaum, Rachel, and Barbara Fidler. 2005. "Commentary on Epstein and Madsen's 'Joint Custody with a Vengeance: The Emergence of Parallel Parenting orders.'" *Canadian Family Law Quarterly* 24: 337–49.

Birnbaum, Rachel, and Willson McTavish. 2001. *Post-Separation Visitation Disputes: Differential Interventions*. Ottawa: Department of Justice Canada.

Bisnaire, Lise, Philip Firestone, and David Rynard. 1990. "Factors Associated with Academic Achievement in Children Following Parental Separation." *American Journal of Orthopsychiatry* 60 (1): 67–76.

Bjarnason, Thoroddur, and Arsaell M. Arnarsson. 2010. "Life Satisfaction Among Children in Different Family Structures: A Comparative Study of 36 Western Countries." *Children and Society* 26: 51–62.

– 2012. "Joint Physical Custody and Communication with Parents: A Cross-National Study of Children in 36 Western Countries." *Journal of Comparative Family Studies* 26: 871–90.

Black, Michele C., Kathleen C. Basile, Matthew J. Breiding, Sharon G. Smith, Mikel L. Walters, Melissa T. Merrick, and Mark R. Stevens.

2011. *The National Intimate Partner and Sexual Violence Survey: 2010 Summary Report.* Atlanta, GA: National Center for injury Prevention and Control, Centers for Disease Control and Prevention.

Blankenhorn, David. 1995. *Fatherless America: Confronting Our Most Urgent Social Problem.* New York: Basic Books.

Bonach, Kathryn. 2005. "Factors Contributing to Quality Coparenting: Implications for Family Policy." *Journal of Divorce and Remarriage* 43 (3/4): 79–103.

Booth, Alan. 1999. "Causes and Consequences of Divorce: Reflections on Recent Research." In *The Postdivorce Family,* edited by Robert A. Thompson and Paul R. Amato, 29–48. Thousand Oaks, CA: Sage.

Booth, Alan, Mindy Scott, and Valarie King. 2010. "Father Residence and Adolescent Problem Behaviour." *Journal of Family Issues* 3: 585–605.

Boyd, Susan. 2003. *Child Custody, Law, and Women's Work.* Toronto: Oxford University Press.

Braver, Sanford L., and E. O'Connell. 1998. *Divorced Dads: Shattering the Myths.* New York: Tarcher/Putnam.

Braver, Sanford L. and D. Stockburger. 2005. "Child Support Guidelines and the Equalization of Living Standards." In *The Law and Economics of Child Support Payments,* edited by William S. Comanor, 91–127. New York: Edward Elgar Publishing.

Braver, Sanford L., Peter Salem, Jessica Pearson, and Stephanie R. DeLuse. 1996. "The Content of Divorce Education Programs: Results of a Survey." *Family and Conciliation Courts Review* 34 (1): 41–59.

Braver, Sanford, Ira Ellman, Ashley Votruba, and William Fabricius. 2011. "Lay Judgments About Child Custody after Divorce." *Psychology, Public Policy and Law* 17: 212–38.

Breivik, Kyrre and Dan Olweus. 2006. "Adolescents' Adjustment in Four Family Structures." *Journal of Divorce and Remarriage* 44: 99–124.

Brinig, Margaret. 2001. "Feminism and Child Custody Under Chapter Two of the American Law Institute's Principles of the Law of Family Dissolution." *Duke Journal of Gender Law and Policy* 8: 310–21.

Brinig, Margaret, and Douglas Allen. 2000. "These Boots Are Made for Walking: Why Most Divorce Filers Are Women." *American Economics and Law Review* 2 (1): 126–69.

Brinkerhoff, Merlin and Eugen Lupri. 1988. "Interspousal Violence." *Canadian Journal of Sociology* 13: 407–34.

British Columbia Family Law Act, SBC 2011, C 25

British Columbia Justice Review Task Force. 2005. *A New Justice System for Children and Families.* Victoria: Ministry of the Attorney General.

Brotsky, Muriel, Susan Steinman, and Steven Zemmelman. 1988. "Joint Custody Through Mediation Reviewed." *Conciliation Courts Review* 26: 53–8.

Brown, Grant A. 2004. "Gender As a Factor in the Response of the Law-enforcement System to Violence Against Partners." *Sexuality and Culture* 8 (3/4): 3–139.

Buchanan, Christy M., Eleanor E. Maccoby, and Sanford M. Dornbusch. 1996. *Adolescents after Divorce.* Cambridge, Mass: Harvard University Press.

Burgoyne, Jacqueline J. L., Roger Ormrod, and Martin Richards. 1987. *Divorce Matters.* London: Penguin Books.

Burke, Peter J., Jan Stets, and Maureen A. Pirog-Good. 1988. "Gender Identity, Self-Esteem, and Physical and Sexual Abuse in Dating Relationships." *Social Psychology Quarterly* 51: 272–85.

Buzawa, Eve S., Thomas L. Austin, James Bannon, and James Jackson. 1992. "Role of Victim Preference in Determining Police Response to Victims of Domestic Violence." In *Domestic Violence: The Changing Criminal Justice Response,* edited by Eve S. Buzawa and Carl G.Buzawa, 255–69. Westport, CT: Auburn House.

Campana, Kathryn, Sandra Henderson, Arnold Stolberg, and Lisa Schum. 2008. "Parenting Maternal and Paternal Parenting Styles, Child Custody and Children's Emotional Adjustment to Divorce." *Journal of Divorce and Remarriage* 48: 1–20.

Canadian Bar Association, National Family Law Section. 2010. *In the Interests of Children.* Ottawa: Canadian Bar Association.

Capaldi, Deborah, Marion Forgatch, and Lynn Crosby. 1994. "Affective Expression in Family Problem Solving with Adolescent Boys." *Journal of Adolescent Research* 9: 28–49.

Carlson, Marcia. 2006. "Family Structure, Father Involvement and Adolescent Outcomes." *Journal of Marriage and Family* 68: 137–54.

Cashmore, Judith, and Patrick Parkinson. 2010. *Shared Care Parenting Arrangements Since the 2006 Family Law Reforms*. Sydney: University of New South Wales Social Research Centre.

Cawson, Pat. 2002. *Child Maltreatment in the Family*. London: NSPCC.

Chase-Lansdale, P. Lindsay, Andrew J. Cherlin, and Kathleen Kiernan. 1995. "The Long-Term Effects of Parental Divorce on the Mental Health of Young Adults: A Developmental Perspective." *Child Development* 66: 1614–34.

Cheriton, Glenn. 1998. *Child Support, Divorce, Custody and Access, and Government Policies*. Ottawa: Commoners Publishing.

Chisolm, Richard. 2009. *Family Courts Violence Review*. Canberra: Department of the Attorney General.

Clarke-Stewart, K. Alison, and Craig Hayward. 1996. "Advantages of Father Custody and Contact for the Psychological Well-Being of School-Age Children." *Journal of Applied Developmental Psychology* 17 (2): 239–70.

Coates, Christine A., Robin Deutsch, Hugh Starnes, Matthew J. Sullivan, and BeaLisa Sydlik. 2004. "Parenting Coordination for High Conflict Families." *Family Court Review* 42 (2): 246–62.

Cobley, Cathy. 2006. "The Quest for Truth: Substantiating Allegations of Physical Abuse in Criminal Prosecutions and Care Proceedings." *International Journal of Law, Policy and the Family* 20: 317–43.

Cohen, Jonathan and Nikki Gershbain. 2001. "For the Sake of the Fathers? Child Custody Reform and the Perils of Maximum Contact." *Canadian Family Law Quarterly* 19 (1): 121–83.

Coley, Rebekah Levine, and Bethany L. Medeiros. 2007. "Reciprocal Longitudinal Relations Between Nonresident Father Involvement and Adolescent Delinquency." *Child Development* 78: 132–47.

Coogler, O. J. 1978. *Structured Mediation in Divorce Settlement*. Lexington, MA: Lexington Books.

Corneau, Guy. 1991. *Absent Fathers, Lost Sons*. Boston: Shambhala.

Cossman, Brenda. 2001. *An Analysis of Options for Changes in the Legal Regulation of Child Custody and Access*. Ottawa: Department of Justice.

Crosbie-Burnett, Margaret. 1991. "Impact of Joint Versus Sole Custody and Quality of the Coparental Relationship on Adjustment of Adolescents in Remarried Families." *Behavioral Sciences and the Law* 9: 439–49.

Crowder, Kyle and Jay Teachman. 2004. "Do Residential Conditions Explain the Relationship Between Living Arrangements and Adolescent Behavior?" *Journal of Marriage and Family* 66: 721–38.

Daly, Martin, and Margo Wilson. 1988. *Homicide*. New York: Aldine De Gruyter.

Dawson, Deborah A. 1991. "Family Structure and Children's Health and Well-Being." *Journal of Marriage and the Family* 53: 573–84.

Department of Justice Canada. 1990. *Evaluation of the Divorce Act, Phase II: Monitoring and Evaluation*, Ottawa: Minister of Justice.

– 2005. *The Child-centred Family Justice Strategy*. Ottawa: Minister of Justice.

Derevensky, Jeffrey L., and Lisa Deschamps. 1997. "Young Adults from Divorced and Intact Families: Perceptions About Preferred Custodial Arrangements." *Journal of Divorce and Remarriage* 27: 105–22.

Drill, Rebecca L. 1986. "Young Adult Children of Divorced Parents: Depression and the Perception of Loss." *Journal of Divorce* 10 (1/2): 169–87.

Dunlop, Rosemary, Ailsa Burns, and Suzanne Bermingham. 2001. Parent-Child Relations and Adolescent Self Image Following Divorce. *Journal of Youth and Adolescence* 30: 117–34.

Dutton, Donald G. 2005a. "Domestic Abuse Assessment in Child Custody Disputes: Beware the Domestic Violence Research Paradigm." *Journal of Child Custody* 2 (4): 23–42.

– 2005b. "On Comparing Apples with Apples Deemed Non-existent: A Reply to Johnson." *Journal of Child Custody* 2 (4): 53–63.

– 2006a. *Rethinking Domestic Violence*. Vancouver: UBC Press.

– 2006b. "A Briefer Reply to Johnson: Re-affirming the Necessity of a Gender Neutral Approach to Custody Evaluations." *Journal of Child Custody* 3 (1): 28–30.

– 2010. "The Gender Paradigm and the Architecture of Antiscience." *Partner Abuse* 1 (1): 5–25.

Dutton, Donald G., and Tonia L. Nichols. 2005. "The Gender Paradigm in Domestic Violence Research and Theory: Part 1 – the

Conflict of Theory and Data." *Aggression and Violent Behavior* 10: 680–714.

Ehrensaft, Miriam K., Terrie E. Moffitt, and Avshalom Caspi. 2004. "Clinically Abusive Relationships in An Unselected Birth Cohort: Men's and Women's Participation and Developmental Antecedents." *Journal of Abnormal Psychology* 113 (2): 258–70.

Elliott, Jane, and Martin Richards. 1985. "Parental Divorce and the Life Chances of Children." *Family Law* 19: 481–4.

Ellis, Bruce J., John Bates, Kenneth A. Dodge, D. M. Fergusson, J. Horwood, Gregory S. Pettit, and Lianne Woodward. 2003. "Does Father Absence Place Daughters at Special Risk for Early Sexual Activity and Teenage Pregnancy?" *Child Development* 74: 801–21.

Ellis, Desmond, and Loretta Wight-Peasley. 1986. *Wife Abuse Among Separated Women*. Paper Presented at the Meeting of the International Association for the Study of Aggression, Chicago.

Ellis, Elizabeth M. 2005. "Help for the Alienated Parent." *American Journal of Family Therapy* 33: 415–26.

Elster, Jon. 1987. "Solomonic Judgments: Against the Best Interest of the Child." *The University of Chicago Law Review* 54 (1): 1–45.

Ely, Margaret, Patrick West, Helen Sweeting, and Martin Richards. 2000. "Teenage Family Life, Life Chances, Lifestyles and Health: A Comparison of Two Contemporary Cohorts." *International Journal of Law, Policy and the Family* 14: 1–30.

Emery, Robert. E. 1999. "Postdivorce Family Life for Children: An Overview of Research and Some Implications for Policy." In *The Postdivorce Family*, edited by R. A. Thompson and P. R. Amato, 3–27. Thousand Oaks, CA: Sage.

– 2007. "Rule or Rorschach?: Approximating Children's Best Interests." *American Journal of Family Therapy* 1 (2): 132–4.

– 1994. *Children of Divorce*. New York: Guilford.

Emery, Robert E., R.K. Otto, and W.T. O'Donohue. 2005. "A Critical Assessment of Child Custody Evaluations." *Psychological Science in the Public Interest* 6: 1–29.

Evenson, Ranae J., and Robin W. Simon. 2005. "Clarifying the Relationship Between Parenthood and Depression." *Journal of Health and Social Behavior* 46: 341–58.

Fabricius, William V. 2003. "Listening to Children of Divorce: New Findings That Diverge from Wallerstein, Lewis, and Blakeslee." *Family Relations* 52 (4): 385–96.

Fabricius, William V., and Jeff A. Hall. 2000. "Young Adults' Perspectives on Divorce: Living Arrangements." *Family and Conciliation Courts Review* 38: 446–61.

Fabricius, William V., and Linda J. Luecken. 2007. "Postdivorce Living Arrangements, Parent Conflict, and Long-Term Physical Health Correlates for Children of Divorce." *Journal of Family Psychology* 21 (2): 195–205.

Fabricius, William V., Sanford L. Braver, Priscila Diaz, and Clorinda E. Velez. 2010. "Custody and Parenting Time: Links to Family Relationships and Well-being after Divorce." In *The Role of the Father in Child Development,* 5th ed., edited by Michael E. Lamb, 201–40. Cambridge: Wiley.

Fabricius, William V., Priscila Diaz, and Sanford L. Braver. 2012. "Parenting Time, Parent Conflict, Parent-Child Relationships, and Children's Physical Health after Divorce." In *Parenting Plan Evaluations: Applied Research for the Family Court,* edited by Kathryn Kuehnle and Leslie Drozd, 100–30. New York: Oxford University Press.

Federal-Provincial-Territorial Family Law Committee. 2002. *Putting Children First: Report on Custody and Access and Child Support.* Ottawa: Government of Canada.

Fidler, Barbara, and Nicholas Bala. 2010. "Children Resisting Postseparation Contact with a Parent: Concepts, Controversies, and Conundrums." *Family Court Review* 48 (1): 10–47.

Fiebert, Martin. 2004. "References Examining Assaults By Women on Their Spouses or Male Partners: An Annotated Bibliography." *Sexuality and Culture* 8 (3/4): 140–77.

Finley, Gordon, and Seth Schwartz. 2007. "Fatherhood Involvement and Long-Term Young Adult Outcomes: The Differential Contributions of Divorce and Gender." *Family Court Review* 45: 573–87.

Firestone, Gregory, and Janet Weinstein. 2004. "In the Best Interests of Children: A Proposal to Transform the Adversarial System." *Family Court Review* 42 (2): 203–15.

Flood-Page, Claire, Siobhan Campbell, Victoria Harrington, and Joel Miller. 2000. *Youth Crime: Findings from the 1998/99 Youth Lifestyles Survey*. London: Home Office Research, Development and Statistics Directorate.

Flouri, Eirini. 2005. *Fathering and Child Outcomes*. Hoboken, NJ: Wiley.

Fox, Greer Litton, and Robert F. Kelly. 1995. "Determinants of Child Custody Arrangements at Divorce." *Journal of Marriage and the Family* 57 (3): 693–708.

Freeman, Michael. 1997. "Divorce Gospel Style." *Family Law* 27: 413–18.

French Ministry of Justice. 2001. Accessed at http://www.justice.gc.ca/eng/pi/fcy-fea/lib-bib/rep-rap/2002/flc2002/flc2002n.html#ftn150.

Friedlander, Steven, and Marjorie. G. Walters. 2010. "When a Child Rejects a Parent: Tailoring the Intervention to Fit the Problem." *Family Court Review* 48 (1): 98–111.

Frost, Abbie K., and Bilge Pakiz. 1990. "The Effects of Marital Disruption on Adolescents: Time As a Dynamic." *American Journal of Orthopsychiatry* 60 (4): 544–55.

Galinsky, Ellen, Kerstin Aumann, and James T. Bond. 2009. *Gender and Generation at Work and at Home*. New York: Families and Work Institute.

Garber, Benjamin. 2004. "Directed Co-parenting Intervention: Conducting Child-Centered Interventions in Parallel with Highly Conflicted Co-parents." *Professional Psychology: Research and Practice* 35 (1): 55–64.

Gilmour, Glenn. 2002. *High Conflict Separation and Divorce: Options for Consideration*. Ottawa: Department of Justice Canada.

Government of Canada. 1985. Divorce Act. R.S.C. 1985 (2nd Supp.): C.3.

Graham, John, and Benjamin Bowling. 1995. *Young People and Crime*. London: Home Office.

Grych, John H. 2005. "Interparental Conflict As a Risk Factor for Child Maladjustment: Implications for the Development of Prevention Programs." *Family Court Review* 43 (1): 97–108.

Gunnoe, Marjorie L., and Sanford L. Braver. 2001. "The Effects of Joint Legal Custody on Mothers, Fathers, and Children Controlling for Factors That Predispose a Sole Maternal Versus Joint Legal Award." *Law and Human Behavior* 25 (1): 25–43.

– 2002. *The Effects of Joint Legal Custody on Family Functioning.* Washington, DC: National Institute of Mental Health.

Hampton, Robert L., Richard J. Gelles, and John W. Harrop. 1989. "Is Violence in Families Increasing? A Comparison of 1975 and 1985 National Survey Rates." *Journal of Marriage and the Family* 51: 969–80.

Hart, Amanda S., and Dale Bagshaw. 2008. "The Idealized Post-separation Family in Australian Family Law: A Dangerous Paradigm in Cases of Domestic Violence." *Journal of Family Studies* 14: 291–309.

Harvey, John, and Mark Fine. 2010. *Children of Divorce.* New York: Routledge.

Haugen, Gry Mette D. 2010. "Children's Perspectives on Shared Residence." *Children and Society* 24: 112–22.

Hawthorne, Bruce, and Christopher J. Lennings. 2008. "The Marginalization of Nonresident Fathers: Their Postdivorce Roles." *Journal of Divorce and Remarriage* 49 (3/4): 191–209.

Healy, Joseph M., Janet E. Malley, and Abibgail J. Stewart. 1990. "Children and Their Fathers after Parental Separation." *American Journal of Orthopsychiatry* 60: 531–43.

Hearn, Jeff. 2002. "Men, Fathers, and the State: National and Global Relations." In *Making Men Into Fathers: Men, Masculinities and the Social Politics of Fatherhood*, edited by Barbara Hobson, 245–72. Cambridge: Cambridge University Press.

Hetherington, E. Mavis, and Joan Kelly. 2002. *For Better or for Worse: Divorce Reconsidered.* New York: Norton.

Hetherington, E. Mavis, Martha Cox, and Roger Cox. 1978. "The Aftermath of Divorce." In *Mother-Child, Father-Child Relations*, edited by Joseph H. Stevens, Jr. and Marilyn Mathews, 149–76. Washington: National Association for the Education of Young Children.

Higgins, Christopher, and Linda Duxbury. 2002. *The 2001 National Work-Life Conflict Study.* Ottawa: Health Canada.

– 2012. *The 2012 National Study on Balancing Work and Caregiving in Canada.* Ottawa: Health Canada.

Hilton, Jeanne M., and Esther L. Devall. 1998. "Comparison of Parenting and Children's Behavior in Single-Mother, Single-Father, and Intact Families." *Journal of Divorce and Remarriage* 29 (3/4): 23–50.

Holmes, William C. 2007. "Men's Childhood Sexual Abuse Histories By One-Parent Versus Two-Parent Status of Childhood Home." *Journal of Epidemiology and Community Health* 61 (4): 319–25.

Hope, Steven, Chris Power, and Bryan Rodgers. 1998. "The Relationship Between Parental Separation in Childhood and Problem Drinking in Adulthood." *Addiction* 93 (4): 505–14.

Horwitz, Sarah, Julia R. Irwin, Margaret J. Briggs-Gowan, Joan M. Bosson Heenan, Jennifer Mendoza, and Alice S. Carter. 2003. "Language Delay in a Community Cohort of Young Children." *Journal of the American Academy of Child and Adolescent Psychiatry* 42: 932–40.

Hotton, Tina. 2001. *Spousal Violence after Marital Separation.* Ottawa: Statistics Canada.

– 2003. "Childhood Aggression and Exposure to Violence in the Home." Crime and Justice Research Paper Series. Catalogue No. 85-561-MIE2003002. Ottawa: Statistics Canada, Canadian Centre for Justice Statistics.

House of Representatives Standing Committee on Family and Community Affairs (FCAC). 2003. *Every Picture Tells a Story: Report of the inquiry Into Child Custody Arrangements in the Event of Family Separation.* Sydney: FCAC.

Irving, Howard H., and Michael Benjamin. 1995. *Family Mediation: Contemporary Issues.* Thousand Oaks, CA: Sage.

Jablonska, Beata, and Lene Lindberg. 2007. "Risk Behaviors and Mental Distress Among Adolescents in Different Family Structures." *Social Psychiatry and Epidemiology* 42: 656–63.

Jacobs, Nicky, and Russell Jaffe. 2010. "Investigating the Efficacy of CoMeT, a New Mediation Model for High-conflict Couples." *American Journal of Family Therapy* 38 (1): 16–31.

Jaffe, Peter, Claire V. Crooks, and Nicholas Bala. 2005. *Making Appropriate Parenting Arrangements in Family Violence Cases: Applying the Literature to Identify Promising Practices.* Ottawa: Department of Justice Canada.

Jaffe, Peter, Nancy Lemon, and Samantha E. Poisson. 2003. *Child Custody and Domestic Violence: A Call for Safety and Accountability.* Thousand Oaks: Sage.

Jenkins, Brian. 2006. *Review of the Attorney General of Canada's Recent Supreme Court Appointees.* Unpublished Paper.

Jeynes, William H. 2000. "A Longitudinal Analysis on the Effects of Remarriage Following Divorce on the Academic Achievement of Adolescents." *Journal of Divorce and Remarriage* 33: 131–48.

– 2001. "The Effects of Recent Parental Divorce on their Children's Consumption of Marijuana and Cocaine." *Journal of Divorce and Remarriage* 35 (3/4): 43–64.

Johnson, Holly, and Tina Hotton. 2003. "Losing Control: Homicide Risk in Estranged and Intact Intimate Relationships." *Homicide Studies* 7 (1): 58–84.

Johnson, Michael P. 2005. "Apples and Oranges in Child Custody Disputes: Intimate Terrorism Versus Situational Couple Violence." *Journal of Child Custody* 2 (4): 43–52.

Johnston, Janet, and Linda E.G. Campbell. 1993. "Parent-Child Relationships in Domestic Violence Families Disputing Custody." *Family and Conciliation Courts Review* 31 (3): 282–98.

Johnston, Janet, Soyoung Lee, Nancy W. Olesen, and Marjorie G. Walters. 2005. "Allegations and Substantiations of Abuse on Custody-Disputing Families." *Family Court Review* 40 (2): 283–94.

Johnston, Janet, Vivienne Roseby, and Kathryn Kuehnle. 2009. *In the Name of the Child: Understanding and Helping Children of Conflicted and Violent Divorce.* New York: Springer.

Johnston, Janet, Marsha Kline, and Jeanne M. Tschann. 1989. "Ongoing Postdivorce Conflict: Effects on Children of Joint Custody and Frequent Access." *American Journal of Orthopsychiatry* 59: 576–92.

Juby, Heather, Nicole Marcil-Gratton, and Celine Le Bourdais. 2004. *When Parents Separate: Further Findings from the National Longitudinal Survey of Children and Youth.* Ottawa: Department of Justice.

Kalter, Neil. 1987. "Long-Term Effects of Divorce on Children: A Developmental Vulnerability Model." *American Journal of Orthopsychiatry* 57 (4): 587–600.

Kaspiew, Rae, Matthew Gray, Ruth Weston, Lawrence Moloney, and
    Lixia Qu. 2009. *Evaluation of the 2006 Family Law Reforms.*
    Melbourne: Australian Institute of Family Studies.
– 2010. "The Australian Institute of Family Studies' Evaluation of the
    2006 Family Law Reforms: Key Findings." *Australian Journal of
    Family Law* 24 (1): 5–33.
Kelly, Joan. 1991. "Examining Resistance to Joint Custody." In *Joint
    Custody and Shared Parenting,* 2nd ed., edited by Jay Folberg and
    Alison Taylor, 55–62. New York: Guilford Press.
– 2000. "Children's Adjustment in Conflicted Marriage and Divorce:
    A Decade Review of Research." *Journal of the American Academy
    of Child and Adolescent Psychiatry* 39: 963–73.
– 2003. "Changing Perspectives on Children's Adjustment Following
    Divorce." *Childhood* 10 (2): 237–54.
– 2004. "Family Mediation Research: Is there Empirical Support for
    the Field?" *Conflict Resolution Quarterly* 22 (1–2): 3–35.
– 2005. "Developing Beneficial Parenting Plan Models for Children
    Following Separation and Divorce." *Journal of the American
    Academy of Matrimonial Lawyers* 19: 237–54.
– 2007. "Children's Living Arrangements Following Separation and
    Divorce: Insights from Empirical and Clinical Research." *Family
    Process* 46 (1): 35–52.
– 2010. "Commentary on Family Bridges." *Family Court Review* 48 (1).
Kelly, Joan, and Janet Johnston. 2005. "Empirical and Ethical Problems
    with Custody Recommendations." *Family Court Review* 43: 233–41.
Kelly, Joan, and Michael Lamb. 2000. "Using Child Development
    Research to Make Appropriate Custody and Access Decisions for
    Young Children." *Family and Conciliation Courts Review* 38 (3):
    297–311.
Kelly, Robert F., and Shawn L. Ward. 2002. "Allocating Custodial
    Responsibilities at Divorce: Social Science Research and the
    American Law Institute's Approximation Rule." *Family Court
    Review* 40: 350–70.
Kiernan, Kathleen. 1997. *The Legacy of Parental Divorce: Social,
    Economic, and Family Experiences in Adulthood.* London: Centre
    for Analysis of Social Exclusion, London School of Economics.

King, Valarie, and Juliana M. Soboleski. 2006. "Nonresident Fathers' Contributions to Adolescent Well-Being." *Journal of Marriage and Family* 68: 537–57.

Kitzmann, Katherine M., Noni Gaylord, Aimee Holt, and Erin Kenny. 2003. "Child Witnesses to Domestic Violence: A Meta-analytic Review." *Journal of Consulting and Clinical Psychology* 71 (2): 339–52.

Kposowa, Augustine. 2000. "Marital Status and Suicide in the National Longitudinal Mortality Study." *Journal of Epidemiology and Community Health* 54 (4): 254–61.

– 2003. "Divorce and Suicide Risk." *Journal of Epidemiology and Community Health* 57: 993–5.

Kruk, Edward. 1991. "The Grief Reaction of Noncustodial Fathers Subsequent to Divorce." *Men's Studies Review* 8 (2): 17–21.

– 1992. "Psychological and Structural Factors Contributing to the Disengagement of Noncustodial Fathers after Divorce." *Family and Conciliation Courts Review* 29 (2): 81–101.

– 1993a. "Promoting Cooperative Parenting after Separation: A Therapeutic /Interventionist Model of Family Mediation." *Journal of Family Therapy* 15 (3): 235–61.

– 1993b. *Divorce and Disengagement.* Halifax: Fernwood.

– 2008. *Child Custody, Access, and Parental Responsibility: The Search for a Just and Equitable Standard.* Guelph: Fatherhood Involvement Research Alliance, Social Science and Humanities Research Council of Canada.

– 2010a. "Parental and Social Institutional Responsibilities to Children's Needs in the Divorce Transition: Fathers' Perspectives." *Journal of Men's Studies* 18 (2): 159–78.

– 2010b. "Collateral Damage: The Lived Experiences of Divorced Mothers without Custody." *Journal of Divorce and Remarriage* 51 (7/8): 526–43.

– 2011. "The Disappearance of Parents from Children's Lives: The Cumulative Effects of Child Care, Child Custody, and Child Protection Policies." In *The End of Children*, edited by G. Allen and N. Lauster, 121–39. Vancouver: University of British Columbia Press.

- 2013. "Social Justice, Spirituality, and Responsibility to Needs: The 'Best Interests of the Child' in the Divorce Transition." *Journal of Spirituality in Mental Health* 15 (2): 94–106.

L'Heureux-Dube, Claire. 1998. "A Response to Remarks by Dr. Judith Wallerstein on the Long-Term Impact of Divorce on Children." *Family and Conciliation Courts Review* 36: 384–91.

Lamb, Michael. E. 1999. "Non-custodial Fathers and Their Impact on Children of Divorce." In *The Post-Divorce Family: Research and Policy Issues*, edited by Ross A. Thompson and Paul R. Amato, 105–25. Thousand Oaks, CA: Sage.

- 2004. "Divorce and Parenting." In *Encyclopedia of Applied Developmental Science,* edited by Celia B. Fisher and Richard M. Lerner, 794–6. New York: Sage.

- 2007. "The Approximation Rule: Another Proposed Reform That Misses the Target." *American Journal of Family Therapy* 1 (2): 135–6.

- 2010. The *Role of the Father in Child Development,* 5th ed. Cambridge: Wiley.

Lamb, Michael E., C. Philip Hwang, Robert Ketterlinus, and Maria P. Fracasso. 1999. "Parent-Child Relationships." In *Developmental Psychology: An Advanced Textbook,* 4th ed., edited by Marc H. Bornstein and Michael E. Lamb, 411–50. Mahwah, NJ: Lawrence Erlbaum.

Lamb, Michael E., Kathleen Sternberg, and Ross A. Thompson. 1997. "The Effects of Divorce and Custody Arrangements on Children's Behavior, Development, and Adjustment." *Family and Conciliation Courts Review* 35: 393–404.

Lamb, Michael E., and Joan Kelly. 2001. "Using the Empirical Literature to Guide the Development of Parenting Plans for Young Children." *Family Court Review* 39 (4): 365–71.

- 2009. "Improving the Quality of Parent-Child Contact in Separating Families with Infants and Young Children." In *The Scientific Basis of Child Custody Decisions,* 2nd ed., edited by Robert M. Galazter-Levy, Louis Kraus, and Jeanne Galatzer-Levy, 187–214. Hoboken, NJ: Wiley.

Laroche, Denis. 2005. *Aspects of the Context and Consequences of Domestic Violence: Situational Couple Violence and Intimate Terrorism in Canada in 1999.* Quebec City: Government of Quebec.

Laumann-Billings, Lisa and Robert E. Emery. 2000. "Distress Among Young Adults from Divorced Families." *Journal of Family Psychology* 14 (4): 671–87.

LeBourdais, Celine, Heather Juby, and Nicole Marcil-Gratton. 2001. *Keeping Contact with Children: Assessing the Father/Child Post-separation Relationship from the Male Perspective.* Ottawa: Department of Justice.

Lebow, Jay. 2003. "Integrative Family Therapy for Disputes Involving Child Custody and Visitation." *Journal of Family Psychology* 17 (2): 181–92.

Legg, Cecily, Allen Mendell, and Barbara Riemer. 1989. "Clinical Observations on Interferences of Early Father Absence in the Achievement of Femininity." *Clinical Social Work Journal* 17 (4).

Lund, Mary. 1987. "The Non-custodial Father : Common Challenges in Parenting after Divorce." In *Reassessing Fatherhood*, edited by Charlie Lewis and Margaret O'Brien, 212–24. London: Sage Publications

Lundbert, Olle. 1993. "The Impact of Childhood Living Conditions on Illness and Mortality in Adulthood." *Social Science and Medicine 36*: 1047–52.

Lupri, Eugen and Elaine Grandin. 2004. *Intimate Partner Abuse Against Men.* Ottawa: National Clearinghouse on Family Violence.

Maccoby, Eleanor, and Robert Mnookin. 1992. *Dividing the Child: Social and Legal Dilemmas of Custody.* Cambridge, MA: Harvard University Press.

Maccoby, Eleanor, Charlene E. Depner, and Robert Mnookin. 1988. "Custody of Children Following Divorce." In *Impact of Divorce, Single Parenting, and Step Parenting on Children*, edited by E. Mavis Hetherington and Josephine D. Arasteh, 325–68. Hillside, NJ: Erlbaum.

Magdol, Lynn, Terrie E. Moffitt, Avshalom Caspi, J. Fagan, Denise L. Newman, and Phil A. Silva. 1997. "Gender Differences in Partner Violence in a Birth Cohort of 21-year-olds: Bridging the Gap Between Clinical and Epidemiological Approaches." *Journal of Consulting and Clinical Psychology* 65: 68–78.

Maldonado, Solangel. 2005. "Beyond Economic Fatherhood." *University of Pennsylvania Law Review* 153: 921–50.

Marquardt, Elizabeth. 2005. *Between Two Worlds: Inner Lives of Children of Divorce*. New York: Crown.

Marshall, Kathryn. 2006. "Converging Gender Roles." *Perspectives on Labour and Income* 7 (1): 5–16 (Statistics Canada).

Mason, Mary Ann. 1996. "Read My Lips: Trends in Judiciary Decision-Making in Custody Disputes." *Family Law Quarterly* 31 (2): 215–36.

– 1994. *From Father's Property to Children's Rights*. New York: Columbia University Press.

McIntosh, Jennifer E. 2009. "Legislating for Shared Parenting: Exploring Some Underlying Assumptions." *Family Court Review* 47 (3): 389–400.

McIntosh, Jennifer E. and Robert Chisolm. 2009. "Shared Care and Children's Best Interests in Conflicted Separation." *Australian Family Lawyer* 20 (1): 1–11.

McMunn, Anne M., James Y. Nazroo, Michael G. Marmot, Richard Boreham, and Robert Goodman. 2001. "Children's Emotional and Behavioural Well-Being and the Family Environment: Findings from the Health Survey for England." *Social Science and Medicine* 53: 423–40.

McMurray, Anne, and A.M. Blackmore, 1992. "Influences of Parent-Child Relationships on Non-custodial Fathers." *Australian Journal of Marriage and Family* 14 (3): 151–9.

McNeely, Robert L., Philip W. Cook, and José B. Torres. 2001. "Is Domestic Violence a Gender Issue or a Human Issue?" *Journal of Human Behavior in the Social Environment* 4 (4): 227–51.

McWhinney, Robert. 1995. "The 'Winner-Loser Syndrome': Changing Fashions in the Determination of Child 'Custody'." *Family and Conciliation Courts Review* 33: 298–307.

Melli, Marygold S. and Patricia R. Brown. 2008. "Exploring a New Family Form: The Shared Time Family." *International Journal of Law, Policy and the Family* 22: 231–69.

Melton, Gary B. 1989. *Reforming the Law: Impact of Child Development Research*. New York: Guilford Press.

Meltzer, Howard, Rebecca Gatward, Robert Goodman, and Tamsin Ford. 2000. *Mental Health of Children and Adolescents in Great Britain*. London: The Stationery Office.

Menning, Chadwick. 2006. "Nonresident Fathering and School
    Failure." *Journal of Family Issues* 27: 1356–82.
Millar, Paul. 2009. *The Best Interests of Children: An Evidence-Based
    Approach*. Toronto: University of Toronto Press.
− 2010. "Punishing Our Way Out of Poverty: The Prosecution of
    Child-support Debt in Alberta, Canada." *Canadian Journal of Law
    and Society* 25 (2): 149–65.
Millar, Paul, and Sheldon Goldenberg. 1998. "Explaining Child
    Custody Determination in Canada." *Canadian Journal of Law and
    Society* 13 (2): 209–25.
− 2004. "A Critical Reading of the Evidence on Custody Determina-
    tions in Canada." *Canadian Family Law Quarterly* 21: 425–435.
Mitchell, Ann. 1985 *Children in the Middle*. London: Tavistock.
Moffitt, Terrie E., Avshalom Caspi, Michael Rutter, and Phil A. Silva.
    2001. *Sex Differences in Antisocial Behaviour*. Cambridge:
    Cambridge University Press.
Moloney, Lawrence. 2009. "'Meaningful Relationships' in the Family
    Law Act Amendments of 2006: A Sociolegal Perspective on Fathers,
    Mothers, and the 'Sharing' of Parenting after Separation." *Journal of
    Family Studies* 15 (1): 9–19.
Moyer, Sharon. 2004. *Child Custody Arrangements: Their Characteris-
    tics and Outcomes*. Ottawa: Department of Justice.
Nanos Research. 2009. *Stat Sheet, National Omnibus 200903,
    Parenting*. Retrieved from www.nanosresearch.com.
Nathanson, Paul, and Katherine K. Young. 2012. "But Are the Kids
    Really All Right?" *New Male Studies* 1 (1): 61–82.
Neoh, Jennifer, and David Mellor. 2010. "Shared Parenting: Adding
    Children's Voices." *Journal of Child Custody* 7: 155–75.
Neufeld, Gordon, and Gabor Mate. 2004. *Hold on to Your Kids: Why
    Parents Need to Matter More Than Peers*. Toronto: Alfred A. Knopf.
Nielsen, Linda. 2013. "Shared Residential Custody: Review of the
    Research." *American Journal of Family Law* 27 (1): 61–71.
Nikolina, Natalie. 2012. "The Influence of International Law on the
    Issue of Co-Parenting: Emerging Trends in International and
    European Instruments." *Utrecht Law Review* 8 (1): 122–44.
O'Connor, Pauline. 2002. *Child Access in Canada: Legal Approaches
    and Program Supports*. Ottawa: Department of Justice Canada.

O'Connell, Mary E. 2007. "When Noble Aspirations Fail: Why We Need the Approximation Rule." *American Journal of Family Therapy* 1 (2): 129–31.

O'Neill, Rebecca. 2002. *Experiments in Living: The Fatherless Family.* London: CIVITAS.

Parish, Thomas S. 1987. "Children's Self Concepts: Are they Affected by Parental Divorce and Remarriage?" *Journal of Social Behavior and Personality* 2 (4): 559–62.

Parkinson, Patrick and Judy Cashmore. 2011. "Parenting Arrangements for Young Children: Messages for Research." *Australian Journal of Family Law* 25: 236–57.

Parkinson, Patrick, Judy Cashmore, and Judi Single. 2003. *Adolescents' Views on the Fairness of Parenting and Financial Arrangements.* Sydney: University of Sydney Faculty of Law.

– 2005. "Adolescents' Views on the Fairness of Parent Arrangements after Separation." *Family Court Review* 43: 430–45.

Parliament of Australia. 2006. *Family Law Amendment (Shared Parental Responsibility) Bill 2005.* Canberra: Parliament of Australia.

Pimlott-Kubiak, Sheryl and Lilia M. Cortina. 2003. "Gender, Victimization, and Outcomes: Reconceptualizing Risk." *Journal of Consulting and Clinical Psychology* 71(3): 528–39.

Polikoff, Nancy D. 1982. "Gender and Child Custody Determinations: Exploding the Myths." In *Families, Politics, and Public Policies: A Feminist Dialogue on Women and the State*, edited by Irene Diamond, 183–202. New York: Longman.

Power, Chris, Bryan Rodgers, and Steven Hope. 1999. "Heavy Alcohol Consumption and Marital Status: Disentangling the Relationship in a National Study of Young Adults." *Addiction* 94 (10): 1477–87.

Pruett, Marsha Kline and Tamara D. Jackson. 1999. "The Lawyer's Role During the Divorce Process: Perceptions of Parents, Their Young Children, and Their Attorneys." *Family Law Quarterly* 33: 283–310.

Pruett, Marsha Kline, Kathy Hoganbruen, and Tamara D. Jackson. 2000. "Parents' and Attorneys' Views of the Best Interests of the Child." *Journal of Divorce and Remarriage* 33: 47–63.

Pruett, Marsha Kline, Tamra Y. Williams, Glendessa Insabella, and Todd D. Little. 2003. "Family and Legal Indicators of Child

Adjustment to Divorce Among Families with Young Children."
Journal of Family Psychology 17 (2): 169–80.

Pulkingham, Jane. 1994. "Private Troubles, Private Solutions: Poverty Among Divorced Women and the Politics of Support Enforcement and Child Custody Determination." *Canadian Journal of Law and Society* 9 (2): 73–97.

Rees, Gwyther and Celia Rutherford. 2001. *Home Run: Families and Young Runaways*. London: The Children's Society.

Richardson, Pamela. 2006. *A Kidnapped Mind*. Toronto: Dundurn Press.

Ringbäck Weitoft, Gunilla, Anders Hjern, Bengt Haglund, and Mans Rosén. 2003. "Mortality, Severe Morbidity, and Injury in Children Living with Single Parents in Sweden: A Population-based Study." *The Lancet* 361: 289–95.

Rosenberg, Jeffrey and William B. Wilcox. 2006. *The Importance of Fathers in the Healthy Development of Children*. Washington: US Department of Health and Human Services.

Rutter, Michael. 1995. "Clinical Implication of Attachment Concepts." *Journal of Child Psychology and Psychiatry* 36: 549–71.

Sandler, Irwin, Jonathan Miles, Jeffrey Cookston, and Sanford Braver. 2008. "Effects of Father and Mother Parenting on Children's Mental Health in High- and Low-Conflict Divorces." *Family Court Review* 46 (2): 282–96.

Semple, Noel. 2010. "Whose Best Interests?: Custody and Access Law and Procedure." *Osgood Hall Law Journal* 48 (2): 1–40.

Serbin, Lisa, Dale Stack, Natacha De Genna, Naomi Grunzeweig, Caroline E. Temcheff, Alex E. Schwartzmann, and Jane Ledingham. 2004. "When Aggressive Girls Become Mothers." In *Aggression, Antisocial Behavior and Violence Among Girls*, edited by Martha Putallaz and Karen L. Bierman, 262–85. New York: The Guilford Press.

Shuman, Daniel W. 2002. "The Role of Mental Health Experts in Custody Decisions: Science, Psychological Tests, and Clinical Judgment." *Family Law Quarterly* 36: 135–62.

Shuman, Daniel W., and Alexander S. Berk. 2012. "The Best Interests of the Child and the Daubert and Frye Evidentiary Frameworks." In *Parenting Plan Evaluations: Applied Research for the Family Court,* edited by Kathryn Kuehnle and Leslie Drozd, 563–73. New York: Oxford University Press.

Smart, Carol. 2002. "From Children's Shoes to Children's Voices." *Family Court Review* 40: 307–19.

Smyth, Bruce. 2009. "A 5-Year Retrospective of Shared Care Research in Australia." *Journal of Family Studies* 15: 36–59.

Somerville, Margaret. 2006. *The Ethical Imagination.* Toronto: Anansi Press.

Sommer, Reena. 1994. *Male and Female Partner Abuse: Testing a Diathesis-Stress Model.* Unpublished Doctoral Dissertation. University of Manitoba.

Special Joint House of Commons-Senate Committee on Child Custody and Access. 1998. *For the Sake of the Children.* Ottawa: Government of Canada.

Spiwak, Rae, and Douglas A. Brownridge. 2005. "Separated Women's Risk for Violence: An Analysis of the Canadian Situation." *Journal of Divorce and Remarriage* 43 (3/4): 105–18.

Spruijt, Ed, and Vincent Duindam. 2010. "Joint Physical Custody in the Netherlands and the Well-Being of Children." *Journal of Divorce and Remarriage* 51: 65–82.

Stamps, Leighton E. 2002. "Maternal Preference in Child Custody Decisions." *Journal of Divorce and Remarriage* 37 (1/2): 1–11.

Statistics Canada. 2007. *Divorce in Canada: A Statistical Profile.* Ottawa: Minister of industry.

– 2008. *Family Violence in Canada: A Statistical Profile.* Ottawa: Minister of industry.

– 2011. *General Social Survey, 2010: Overview of the Time Use of Canadians.* Ottawa: Minister of Industry.

Stein, Judith A., Norweeta G. Millburn, Jazmin I. Zane, and Mary Jane Rotheram-Bors. 2009. "Paternal and Maternal Influences on Problem Behaviors Among Homeless and Runaway Youth." *American Journal of Orthopsychiatry* 79 (1): 39–50.

Sternberg, Kathleen J. 1997. "Fathers: The Missing Parents in Research on Family Violence." In *The Role of the Father in Child Development,* 3rd ed, edited by M.E. Lamb, 284–308. New York: Wiley.

Stets, Jan E. and Debra A. Henderson. 1991. "Contextual Factors Surrounding Conflict Resolution While Dating: Results from a National Study." *Family Relations* 40: 29–40.

Stets, Jan E. and Murray A. Straus. 1990. "Gender Differences in Reporting Marital Violence and Its Medical and Psychological Consequences." In *Physical Violence in American Families: Risk Factors and Adaptations to Violence in 8,145 Families,* edited by Murray A. Straus and Richard J. Gelles, 151–66. New Brunswick, NJ: Transaction.

– 1992. *The Marriage License As a Hitting License: Physical Violence in American Families.* New Brunswick, NJ: Transaction Publishers.

Stewart, Ron. 2001. *The Early Identification and Streaming of Cases of High Conflict Separation and Divorce: A Review.* Ottawa: Department of Justice Canada.

Stith, Sandra M., Karen H. Rosen, Eric E. McCollum, and Cynthia J. Thomsen. 2004. "Treating Intimate Partner Violence within Intact Couple Relationships: Outcomes of Multi-couple Versus Individual Couple Therapy." *Journal of Marital and Family Therapy* 30: 305–18.

Straus, Murray A. 1993. "Physical Assaults By Wives: A Major Social Problem." In *Current Controversies on Family Violence*, edited by Donilene R. Loseke, Richard J. Gelles and Mary M. Cavanaugh, 67–87. Newbury Park, CA: Sage.

– 1995. "Trends in Cultural Norms and Rates of Partner Violence: An Update to 1992." In *Understanding Partner Violence: Prevalence, Causes, Consequences, and Solutions,* edited by Sandra M. Stith and Murray A. Straus, 30–3. Minneapolis, MN: National Council on Family Relations.

– 1999. "The Controversy over Domestic Violence By Women: A Methodological, theoretical, and Sociology of Science Analysis." In *Violence in Intimate Relationships*, edited by Ximena B. Arriaga and Stuart Oskamp, 17–44. Thousand Oaks, CA: Sage.

Sudermann, Marlies, and Peter Jaffe. 1998. *A Handbook for Health and Social Service Providers and Educators on Children Exposed to Woman Abuse/Family Violence.* Ottawa: National Clearinghouse on Family Violence.

Sullivan, Matthew J., Peggie A. Ward, and Robin M. Deutsch. 2010. "Overcoming Barriers Family Camp." *Family Court Review* 48 (1): 116–35.

Sweeting, Helen, Patrick West, and Martin Richards. 1998. "Teenage Family Life, Lifestyles and Life Chances: Associations with Family

Structure, Conflict with Parents and Joint Family Activity." *International Journal of Law, Policy and the Family* 12: 15–46.

Swift, Karen and Marilyn Callahan. 2009. *At Risk: Social Justice in Child Welfare.* Toronto: University of Toronto Press.

Taylor, Raymond J. 2005. "Treating Your Divorced Ex-spouse with C.A.R.E.: A Model for Post-Divorce Communication." *Journal of Divorce and Remarriage* 43 (3/4): 157–63.

Tepp, Alan. 1983. "Divorced Fathers: Predictors of Continued Parental involvement." *American Journal of Psychiatry* 140 (11): 1465–9.

Tippins, Timothy M., and Jeffrey P. Wittman. 2005. "Empirical and Ethical Problems with Custody Recommendations: A Call for Clinical Humility and Judicial Vigilance." *Family Court Review* 43 (2): 193–222.

Toews, Michelle L., and Patrick C. McKenry. 2001. "Court-Related Predictors of Parental Cooperation and Conflict after Divorce." *Journal of Divorce and Remarriage* 35 (1/2): 57–73.

Tompkins, Robert. 1995. "Parenting Plans: A Concept Whose Time Has Come." *Family and Conciliation Courts Review* 33: 286–97.

Trinder, L. 2009. "What Might Children Mean by a 'Meaningful Relationship'?" *Journal of Family Studies* 15: 20–35.

Trocme, Nico, and Nicholas Bala. 2005. "False Allegations of Abuse and Neglect When Parents Separate." *Child Abuse and Neglect* 29: 1333–45.

Trocme, Nico, Barbara Fallon, Bruce MacLaurin, Joanne Daciuk, Caroline Felstiner, Tara Black, Lil Tonmyr, Cindy Blackstock, Ken Barter, Daniel Turcotte, and Richard Cloutier. 2005. *Canadian Incidence Study of Reported Child Abuse and Neglect 2003: Major Findings.* Ottawa: Minister of Public Works and Government Services Canada.

Tucker, Joan S., Howard S. Friedman, Joseph E. Schwartz, and Michael H. Criqui. 1997. "Parental Divorce: Effects on Individual Behavior and Longevity." *Journal of Personality and Social Psychology* 73: 381–91.

UNICEF. 2013. *Child Well-Being in Rich Countries.* Florence: UNICEF Innocenti Research Centre.

– 2007. *Child Poverty in Perspective: An Overview of Child Well-Being in Rich Countries.* Florence: UNICEF Innocenti Research Centre.

UK Department for Education 2012. *Co-operative Parenting Following Separation: Proposed Legislation in the involvement of Parents in a Child's Life.* London: Department for Education.

UK Parliament 2012. *Children and Families Bill: Explanatory Notes.* Accessed at http://www.publications.parliament.uk/pa/bills/cbill/2012–2013/0131/en/2013131en.htm.

Vanier Institute for the Family. 2010. *Families Count: Profiling Canada's Families IV.* Ottawa: Vanier Institute for the Family.

Ver Steegh, Nancy, and Clare Dalton. 2008. "Report from the Wingspread Conference on Domestic Violence and Family Courts." *Family Court Review* 46 (3): 454–75.

Walker, Janet. 1993. "Co-operative Parenting Post-divorce: Possibility or Pipedream?" *Journal of Family Therapy* 15 (3): 273–93.

Wallerstein, Judith S. 1991. "The Long-Term Effects of Divorce on Children: A Review." *Journal of the American Academy of Child and Adolescent Psychiatry* 30 (3): 349–60.

Wallerstein, Judith S. and Joan Kelly. 1980. *Surviving the Breakup: How Children and Parents Cope with Divorce.* New York: Basic Books.

Wallerstein, Judith S., Julia Lewis, and Sandra Blakeslee. 2000. *The Unexpected Legacy of Divorce: A 25-Year Landmark Study.* New York: Hyperion.

Warshak, Richard A. 2007. "The Approximation Rule, Child Development Research, and Children's Best Interests after Divorce." *American Journal of Family Therapy* 1 (2): 119–25.

– 1992. *The Custody Revolution.* New York: Simon and Schuster.

– 2003a. "Payoffs and Pitfalls of Listening to Children." *Family Relations* 53: 373–384.

– 2003b. "The Primary Parent Presumption: Primarily Meaningless." In *101+ Practical Solutions for the Family Lawyer: Sensible Answers to Common Problems,* 2nd ed., edited by Gregg M. Herman, 123–5. Chicago: American Bar Association.

– 2010a. *Divorce Poison.* New York: Harper Collins.

– 2010b. "Family Bridges: Using Insights from Social Science to Reconnect Parents and Alienated Children." *Family Court Review* 48 (1): 48–80.

– 2011. "Parenting By the Clock: The Best Interest of the Child Standard and the Approximation Rule." *Baltimore Law Review* 41: 85–163.

Weil, Simone. 1943. *The Need for Roots*. Translated by Arthur Wills. New York: G.P. Putnam.

Wellings, Kaye, Kiran Nanchahal, and Wendy MacDowall. 2001. "Sexual Behaviour in Britain: Early Heterosexual Experience." *The Lancet* 358: 1843–50.

Wellings, Kaye, Julia Field, Anne M. Johnson, Jane Wadsworth, and Sally Bradshaw. 1994. *Sexual Behaviour in Britain*. London: Penguin.

Whitaker, Daniel J., Tadesse Haileyesus, Monica Swahn, and Linda Saltzman. 2007. "Differences in Frequency of Violence and Reported injury Between Relationships with Reciprocal and Nonreciprocal Intimate Partner Violence." *American Journal of Public Health* 97 (5): 941–7.

Whitehead, Denise. 2012. The *Shared Custody Experience: The Adult Child's Perspective on Transitions, Relationships and Fairness*. Unpublished Doctoral Dissertation. University of Guelph.

Wingspread Conference. 2001. "Reforming the System to Protect Children in High Conflict Custody Cases." *Family Court Review* 39 (2): 146–57.

Woodhouse, Barbara B. 1999. "Child Custody in the Age of Children's Rights: The Search for a Just and Equitable Standard." *Family Law Quarterly* 33: 815–32.

Index